AutPlay Therapy for Children and Adolescents on the Autism Spectrum

AutPlay Therapy is a behavioral play-based treatment approach to working with children and adolescents with autism spectrum disorder and other developmental disabilities. This innovative new model contains a parent-training component (wherein the therapist trains parents to do directive play therapy interventions in the home) and can be utilized in any setting where children and adolescents with an autism disorder, ADHD, dysregulation issues, or other neurodevelopmental disorders are treated. This comprehensive resource outlines the AutPlay Therapy process and offers a breakdown of treatment phases along with numerous assessment materials and over 30 directive play therapy techniques.

Robert Jason Grant Ed.D, LPC, CAS, RPT-S is a Licensed Professional Counselor, National Board Certified Counselor, Registered Play Therapist Supervisor, and a Certified Autism Specialist. Dr. Grant is a member of the American Counseling Association, Association for Play Therapy, American Mental Health Counselors Association, and the Autism Society of America. He offers training to become a Certified AutPlay Therapy Provider through his website RobertJasonGrant.com and owns a private practice in Missouri where he works with children, adolescents, adults, couples, and families.

AutPlay Therapy for Children and Adolescents on the Autism Spectrum

A Behavioral Play-Based Approach

Third Edition

Robert Jason Grant

Routledge
Taylor & Francis Group

NEW YORK AND LONDON

First published 2017
by Routledge
711 Third Avenue, New York, NY 10017

and by Routledge
2 Park Square, Milton Park, Abingdon, Oxon, OX14 4RN

*Routledge is an imprint of the Taylor & Francis Group,
an informa business*

First edition published in 2012 by Robert Jason Grant Ed.D
Second edition published in 2014 by Robert Jason Grant Ed.D

Library of Congress Cataloging-in-Publication Data
Names: Grant, Robert Jason, 1971–
Title: Autplay therapy for children and adolescents on the autism
  spectrum : a behavioral play-based approach / Robert Jason Grant.
Other titles: Aut play therapy for children and adolescents on the autism
  spectrum
Description: Third edition. | New York : Routledge, 2016. | Includes
  bibliographical references and index.
Identifiers: LCCN 2015047329 (print) | LCCN 2016000177 (ebook) |
  ISBN 9781138100398 (hardback : alk. paper) | ISBN 9781138100404
  (pbk. : alk. paper) | ISBN 9781315657684 (ebook)
Subjects: LCSH: Play therapy. | Play—Psychological aspects. | Play
  assessment (Child psychology) | Autism in children—Treatment. |
  Autism in adolescence—Treatment. | Autism spectrum disorders in
  children—Treatment. | Autism spectrum disorders—Treatment.
Classification: LCC RJ505.P6 G73 2016 (print) | LCC RJ505.P6 (ebook) |
  DDC 618.92/891653—dc23
LC record available at http://lccn.loc.gov/2015047329

ISBN: 978-1-138-10039-8 (hbk)
ISBN: 978-1-138-10040-4 (pbk)
ISBN: 978-1-315-65768-4 (ebk)

Typeset in Sabon
by Apex CoVantage, LLC

This book is dedicated to all the parents who are bravely and selflessly parenting a child with autism or other developmental disorder. Keep advocating, persevering, and championing for your child. Never forget to care for yourself and never lose faith in your ability to make a difference for your child.

"Don't think that there's a different, better child 'hiding' behind the autism. This is your child. Love the child in front of you. Encourage his strengths, celebrate his quirks, and improve his weaknesses, the way you would with any child. You may have to work harder on some of this, but that's the goal."
—Claire Scovell LaZebnik

Contents

Foreword

Thirty-some years ago, I attended a seminar about how to work with children on the autism spectrum, as well as with their families. It was presented by an individual who was considered an expert at that time. Much of the material was about the use of behavioral approaches, and some of it was quite helpful. What struck me the most, however, was a startling comment made that day. The presenter confidently reported that "behavioral approaches are the only ones that work. These children do not have emotions, but they do respond to operant conditioning methods." At first, I thought I had misheard him, so I asked several other attendees what they had heard. We had all heard the same thing. Although I didn't have experience with ASD at the time, I had been working in the mental health field for several years with children and adults with developmental and emotional challenges. I simply could not accept this statement to be true. It made no sense.

We have learned much in the intervening years. Of course, these children have emotions. Although their developmental trajectory might be atypical, they have the same core social, emotional, and behavioral needs that all people do. Life presents unique challenges for them, and therapists must have a wide range of interventions that they can use to facilitate children's and families' journeys toward reaching their full potential and satisfaction in life.

When a child or adolescent is diagnosed with autism spectrum disorder (ASD), it affects everyone in the family. Family resources must be garnered to learn about ASD, to understand fully the child's or adolescent's specific presentation of ASD, and to determine what treatments are best suited to enhance the family's efforts to ensure as full and as rich a life as possible for all family members. Siblings have their own needs as family energies are diverted toward the care of the child or adolescent with ASD, and parents often carry an additional emotional burden as they try to help their child with ASD while still finding ways to replenish their own energies to meet their own needs as well. Families must sort through the sources of help that are available and frequently are called upon to advocate for their children.

Therapists can be a source of tremendous support and guidance for families struggling to find their way. It is critical, however, that they understand the innumerable ways that ASD can present itself and the significant demands on family life. Therapists must be empathic as well as practical in the help that they offer. They must continuously educate themselves so that they are able to suggest or provide tools that will truly help everyone in the family. They must understand family systems and how a diagnosis of ASD can affect how everyone in the family functions and relates to each other and to others outside the family.

When I first attended a seminar presented by Dr. Robert Grant a number of years ago, I was impressed by his incorporation of a multimodal family model for working with children and adolescents with ASD and their families. In contrast to the seminar I attended all those years ago, there was clear acknowledgment of the behavioral, emotional, social, and developmental components of this challenging disorder. There was also a focus on strengths, i.e., ways that therapists could help identify and build upon the strong points of each individual in the family as well as the family as a whole. His focus on skill building was clearly a way to accomplish this.

This book generously shares what Dr. Grant has learned through the years and provides a clear understanding of ASD. It outlines specific and practical forms of treatment that are guided by an underlying framework based on empathy, family involvement, and understanding the complexities involved. I know of no other resource that so completely helps practitioners understand what ASD is all about and then provides them with myriad tools they can apply with the children and families with whom they work in a wide range of circumstances. It is an important resource, and one that every clinician who works with ASD should have and use. Its thoroughness, embedded in a sensitive, creative, and well-informed approach, is of tremendous value.

If I had to select one resource for clinicians to understand and help children and adolescents with ASD and their families, it would be this one. I hope that this book gets wide readership because, if it does, many families will be assisted in achieving their fullest potential despite the challenges they face when a child has ASD. This is a book about empowerment. Practitioners are empowered by the wealth of information and ideas, and they, in turn, can better empower the parents and children with whom they work.

Albert Einstein wrote, "In the middle of difficulty lies opportunity." This book offers inspirational and practical ways that clinicians can help families find those opportunities.

Risë VanFleet, Ph.D., RPT-S, CDBC
President, Family Enhancement & Play Therapy Center
Boiling Springs, Pennsylvania

Acknowledgments

I want to acknowledge my wife Faith and my family and friends who have been supportive of all my professional efforts; encouraging me, supporting me, and being truly kind and interested in what I am doing. This has meant very much to me, and I thank all of you! A special thanks to my son for excusing me from some serious and important play time to write on this book.

I have had the opportunity to meet many good people in the mental health and autism fields. So many professionals have become friends and so many have inspired, supported, and encouraged me. It makes me hesitant to name any names for fear of forgetting someone, but a special acknowledgment has to go to Joanne Lara, Annette Brandenburg, Dayna Ault, Denise Filley, Tracy Turner-Bumberry, Liana Lowenstein, Rise VanFleet, Audrey Gregan Modikoane, Bill Burns, Deanne Gruenberg, and Gary Yorke. You all have been supportive of me and supportive of AutPlay Therapy. It is much appreciated—thank you!

I want to acknowledge a list of people who have truly inspired me to write, create, and carry forward with my AutPlay efforts. Temple Grandin, Tony Attwood, Carol Gray, Karen Levine, Chantal Sicile-Kira, Eliana Gil, Eric Green, Cherie Spehar, and Terry Kottman. Your writings, presentations, words, and interactions have impacted me in many positive ways—thank you!

A very big appreciation and thanks to all the certified AutPlay Therapy Providers out there! I have been honored by each one of you participating in an AutPlay training and moved by your desire to help improve the lives of children with autism.

Thanks to all of you in my play therapy community. I have enjoyed getting to know each of you and have been inspired by meeting so many of you and continuing to get to know many of you better. Thank you to the Missouri Association for Play Therapy, it has been an honor to be a part of a great board, and I have enjoyed promoting and being a small part.

Thank you to my local autism community! You all are excellent and I am so glad to be a part of a rich and caring community. Southwest Autism Network of Missouri (SWAN), Missouri Autism Report (MAR), and Moms of Children who Have Autism (M.O.C.H.A.), thank you for all your support!

A special thanks to my proofreading, editing friend Wendy Eno. Your thoroughness, attention, and care for the best product have been a blessing and a relief to me.

Finally, I want to acknowledge God, my everything encourager, supporter, and advocate.

Introduction

The process of AutPlay Therapy began several years ago when the first client with autism spectrum disorder came into my office: an elementary school boy who had been diagnosed with Asperger's syndrome. At this point in my career, I was well versed in play therapy approaches, but my knowledge and experience treating individuals with autism disorders were sparse. To say that I did not have success with play therapy approaches would be false. I did have success, and my client made progress, but I was keenly aware that something was missing, that we could be and should be achieving more gains. I was also aware that my involvement with this child's parents was limited in terms of helping his parents with the struggles they were experiencing in themselves and concerns they were having with their child in the home and in school settings.

The parents of this client inspired me a great deal. I felt an instant empathic connection to them. I heard their stories, their struggles, their fears, and I immediately wanted to help. I felt inspired to do something that would make their lives better and improve the quality of experiences for their child, for them, for their whole family. I wanted to increase my own knowledge base so I could be more effective with families that had children with autism spectrum disorder.

It was then that I began a personal journey to become fully educated and trained in the area of autism spectrum disorder and to put myself in a place where I could provide treatment to families that would be effective and supportive. My journey took me to several places, learning many approaches from applied behavioral analysis (ABA) to Floortime, from Social Stories to Pivotal Response Training, from gluten-free diets to animal-assisted therapies, to anything else I could be exposed to and better understand how to help my clients. My knowledge about autism and other developmental disorders increased greatly.

I began to notice a trend in the treatments I was learning; many had elements that mirrored or approximated things I already knew and did in various play therapy approaches. I realized that with a specific autism purpose in mind, a play therapy approach could be created that would be a viable, effective treatment option for both child and parent. I began putting the components together and completing case studies on the clients I was working with. I found that my approach was yielding very positive results for children and families dealing with autism and other developmental disorder issues. The approach grew, and the approach eventually became known as AutPlay Therapy. Process and research continue to improve and AutPlay Therapy continues to grow and evolve as a viable treatment approach for autism and other developmental disorders.

The purpose of this book is to present the practitioner with a thorough understanding of AutPlay Therapy, which provides a comprehensive treatment approach to working with children and adolescents with autism spectrum disorder, other neurodevelopmental disorders, and developmental disabilities. This handbook functions much like a treatment manual by providing a compressive protocol for working with children and adolescents with autism and providing a treatment approach guideline from beginning of treatment to termination.

This handbook provides an overview of autism spectrum disorder and other developmental disabilities, so practitioners can gain a basic knowledge of these complex disorders. Practitioners are encouraged to be continually increasing their knowledge of autism spectrum disorder and other developmental disorders. The AutPlay Therapy process will make the most sense to practitioners who have a thorough understating of autism spectrum disorder.

To effectively implement AutPlay Therapy, it is essential that practitioners be knowledgeable about the various developmental conditions that the practitioner may be working with. A complete understanding and knowledge base in these disorders is imperative to creating the directive play therapy techniques (a central feature in AutPlay Therapy) that are effective in increasing a child's skill development. The AutPlay Therapy handbook by no means provides thorough coverage of autism spectrum disorder and all developmental disorders. The Appendix provides recommended reading to increase a practitioner's knowledge about autism and other developmental disorders.

This handbook presents a review of the influences on AutPlay Therapy, reviewing the established treatments and theories that influenced the creation of AutPlay Therapy. Also, a thorough description of the AutPlay Therapy approach as well as the three phases of AutPlay Therapy, parent-training protocol, AutPlay Therapy research-related information, and several directive play-based interventions that focus on specific skill development are covered.

The Appendix provides several resources for practitioners. Further, many inventories and forms that are used throughout the AutPlay process are explained and provided for practitioner use. The Appendix also lists information about several other play-based treatments for autism spectrum disorder as well as several recommended resources for practitioners and families. The AutPlay Therapy handbook is a comprehensive guidebook for practitioners working with children with autism designed to provide a solid treatment approach from the beginning of treatment to completion of treatment goals.

1 Autism Spectrum Disorder and Developmental Disabilities

Autism Spectrum Disorder Overview

This handbook is not intended to provide a thorough or in-depth presentation of autism spectrum disorder (ASD), neurodevelopmental disorders, and developmental disabilities. Brief information is presented on these areas to help practitioners have a better understanding of such disorders and disabilities as it relates to understanding AutPlay Therapy and implementing directive play-based interventions for treatment. Practitioners are encouraged to engage in continual learning and advancement in their knowledge of ASD and other developmental disorders. To assist in advancement, references and a recommended reading list are presented in the Appendix.

According to the Autism Society of America (2014), autism spectrum disorder (ASD) is a complex developmental disability that typically appears during the first three years of life. ASD is the result of a neurological disorder that affects the normal functioning of the brain. This disorder primarily impacts the normal development of the brain in areas of social interaction and communication skills.

The Centers for Disease Control and Prevention (2015) have proposed that ASD is a developmental disability that can cause significant social, communication, and behavioral challenges. There is often nothing about how people with ASD look that sets them apart from other people, but people with ASD may communicate, interact, behave, and learn in ways that are different from most other people. The learning, thinking, and problem-solving abilities of people with ASD can range from severely challenged to gifted. Some people with ASD need a lot of help in their daily lives; others need far less. A diagnosis of ASD now includes several conditions that used to be diagnosed separately: autistic disorder, pervasive developmental disorder, not otherwise specified (PDD-NOS), and Asperger's syndrome. These conditions are now all called autism spectrum disorder.

Autism spectrum disorder is a *Diagnostic and Statistical Manual,* 5th Edition (2014) diagnosis that is usually given after a thorough psychological evaluation wherein the evaluator measures the child's or adolescent's behavior across a myriad of tests, assessments, and observations. The disorder is a spectrum disorder, meaning the symptoms vary in intensity from severe to very mild. Common terms used to describe the variance include low and high functioning and severe to mild impairment. Children and adolescents with ASD will likely have similar problem areas, but the severity of their difficulty and the presence or absence of other features (fine motor clumsiness, normal intelligence, increased or decreased verbal output) varies (Coplan, 2010).

Children and adolescents with autism spectrum disorder usually have difficulties in verbal and nonverbal communication, social interactions, emotional regulation, and leisure and play skills. Children and adolescents with ASD may also exhibit repeated body movements (hand flapping, rocking), unusual responses to people, or attachments to objects. Children and adolescents with ASD may also have an insistence on sameness, which makes it difficult to make minor changes in personal routines or in the immediate environment (Williams & Williams, 2011). Further, these children and adolescents may have unusual responses to or experience sensitivities in sensory processing. There are typically no physical distinctions or characteristics that set a person with an ASD apart. Children and adolescents with an ASD will likely communicate, interact, behave, and learn in ways that are different from neurotypical peers and different from understood ways of communication, interaction, and learning.

Children and adolescents with autism spectrum disorder may develop their own speech, and comprehension may be poor and the pragmatics or social aspects of language are sometimes lacking. Communication deficits may be varied and include expressive disorder, which leaves comprehension intact; mixed receptive expressive disorders; structural language disorders in which spoken language is impaired; and articulation disorders (Williams & Williams, 2011). In children and adolescents with ASD, receptive language ability is usually low, and expressive language ability is much higher, making it challenging for the child when adults working with the child assume that, because expressive language skills are on par or advanced, then receptive language skills should be at the same level.

Children and adolescents with ASD may perseverate (for example, lining up objects repetitively) and may repeat words in a scripted way or recite whole books that have been read to the child or entire TV shows or movies he or she has seen (Greenspan & Wieder, 2006). The variety and degree of symptoms and conditions associated with an ASD must be noted when working with children and adolescents with this diagnosis, and each individual child and adolescent should be thoroughly assessed for individual issues that are buttressed against appropriate developmental milestones for growth that are age appropriate.

An ASD typically accompanies difficulties in relating and forming relationships, in communicating, and in executive functioning. ASD is a complex developmental disorder. Problems can express themselves differently and can appear in different combinations. Not every child under the same generic diagnostic label has all of these problems to the same degree (Greenspan & Wieder, 2006).

Autism spectrum disorder ranges from severe to mild in terms of impairment on an individual. A child on the severe end of the spectrum may be unable to speak and also have more serious developmental delays. A child on the mild end of the spectrum may be able to function in a regular classroom at school and eventually may reach a point where he or she no longer meets the criteria for ASD. Even if two children have the same diagnosis, no two children with an ASD are alike. One child with an ASD may be nonverbal and have a low IQ, while another child with the same diagnosis may have an above-average IQ, and yet a third child may be verbally and intellectually precocious. Moreover, often the terms "low functioning" and "high functioning" are merely used to describe the child's placement on the autism spectrum (Exkorn, 2005). A more accurate way to view the autism spectrum might be to view each child individually and assess the particular child plotting him or her where he or she currently places in each developmental skill area. Because, in fact, children and adolescents with ASD do not fall into one of two categories—low or high functioning—each child has their own place on the spectrum according to their individual functioning and skill level.

AutPlay Therapy is designed to focus on core deficit areas found in children with ASD, primarily emotional regulation, social interaction, play skills, and relationship attachment and connection. AutPlay Therapy is designed to work with children and adolescents with severe to mild impairment in functioning. The diagnostic criteria for ASD are central to AutPlay Therapy treatment to best understand deficits that a child or adolescent may be experiencing, the level of impairment a child may have, and how to specifically design play therapy techniques to address the child's deficits.

Diagnostic Criteria

Specific diagnosis criteria for autism spectrum disorder (299.00) can be found in the *Diagnostic and Statistical Manual of Mental Disorders*, 5th Edition (DSM-V, 2014). Criteria is categorized and evaluators are required to follow DSM-V procedure, which requires children and adolescents diagnosed with autism spectrum disorder to meet criteria standards in each category presented. The following provides a brief synopsis of the DSM-V diagnostic criteria for autism spectrum disorder:

> Deficits in social-emotional reciprocity, ranging for example, from abnormal social approach and failure of normal back and forth conversation; to reduced sharing of interests, emotions, or affect; to failure to initiate or respond to social interactions. Deficits in nonverbal communication behaviors used for social interaction, ranging, for example, from poorly integrated verbal and nonverbal communication; to abnormalities in eye contact and body language or deficits in understanding and use of gestures; to a total lack of facial expressions and nonverbal communication. Deficits in developing, maintaining, and understanding relationships, ranging, for example, from difficulties adjusting behavior to suit various

social contexts; to difficulties in sharing imaginative play or in making friends; to absence of interest in peers. Stereotyped or repetitive motor movements, use of objects, or speech (simple motor stereotypes, lining up toys or flipping objects, echolalia, idiosyncratic phrases). Insistence on sameness, inflexible adherence to routines, or ritualized patterns of verbal or nonverbal behavior (extreme distress at small changes, difficulties with transitions, rigid thinking patterns, greeting rituals, need to take same route or eat same food every day). Highly restricted, fixated interests that are abnormal in intensity or focus (strong attachment to or preoccupation with unusual objects, excessively circumscribed or perseverative interests). Hyper- or hyporeactivity to sensory input or unusual interest in sensory aspects of the environment (apparent indifference to pain/temperature, adverse response to specific sounds, textures, excessive smelling or touching of objects, visual fascination with lights or movement).

Autism Spectrum Disorder Statistics

Statistics from the Centers for Disease Control and Prevention (2015):

- It is estimated that an average of 1 in 68 children in the United States have autism spectrum disorder.
- Autism spectrum disorder is reported to occur in all racial, ethnic, and socioeconomic groups.
- Autism spectrum disorder is almost 5 times more common among boys (1 in 54) than among girls (1 in 252).
- Autism spectrum disorder tends to occur more often in people who have certain genetic or chromosomal conditions. About 10 percent of children with autism are also identified as having Down syndrome, fragile X syndrome, tuberous sclerosis, and other genetic and chromosomal disorders.
- ASD commonly co-occurs with other developmental, psychiatric, neurologic, chromosomal, and genetic diagnoses. The co-occurrence of one or more non-ASD developmental diagnoses is 83 percent. The co-occurrence of one or more psychiatric diagnoses is 10 percent.
- About 40 percent of children with autism spectrum disorder do not speak at all. Another 25–30 percent of children with autism have some words at 12 to 18 months of age and then lose them. Other children with ASD may speak but not until later in childhood.
- About 1 in 6 children in the U.S. had a developmental disability in 2006–2008, ranging from mild disabilities such as speech and language impairments to serious developmental disabilities, such as intellectual disabilities, cerebral palsy, and autism.
- Almost half (46 percent) of children identified with ASD has average to above-average intellectual ability.
- The median age of earliest ASD diagnosis is between 4.5 and 5.5 years, but for 51–91 percent of children with an ASD, developmental concerns had been recorded before 3 years of age.

- Research has shown that a diagnosis of autism spectrum disorder at age 2 can be reliable, valid, and stable. Despite evidence that ASD can often be identified at around 18 months, many children do not receive final diagnoses until they are much older.
- Studies have shown that many parents of children with autism spectrum disorder notice a developmental problem before their child's first birthday. Concerns about vision and hearing were more often reported in the first year, and differences in social, communication, and fine motor skills were evident from 6 months of age.
- It is estimated to cost at least $17,000 more per year to care for a child with ASD compared to a child without ASD. Costs include health care, education, ASD-related therapy, family-coordinated services, and caregiver time. For a child with more severe ASD, costs per year increase to over $21,000. Taken together, it is estimated that total societal costs of caring for children with ASD were over $9 billion in 2011.

Early Detection of an Autism Spectrum Disorder

The Centers for Disease Control and Prevention has an initiative to help parents and professionals understand and assess for early signs of autism spectrum disorder. Further, the Centers for Disease Control and Prevention also provide information to parents and professionals on appropriate developmental milestones and behaviors. Early detection of an ASD enables the caregiver to begin services for a child at a critical time when the child is in a prime developmental period. While early detection of an ASD usually means that the child is diagnosed between the ages of 1–2 years old, in reality, many children with an ASD are not diagnosed until much later. As noted in the previous statistics section, the average age for an ASD diagnosis is 4.5–5.5, which is too old to qualify for early intervention programs.

When a child is diagnosed with autism spectrum disorder prior to 4 years of age, it provides the opportunity for him or her to be placed into an early intervention program. Most early intervention programs are very successful at treating children with autism disorders and provide a multifaceted approach that helps children make great strides in skill and developmental areas. In fact, research abounds with evidence that early intervention programs, even though there can be great variance in these programs, offer the best route for making critical skill gains (Corsello, 2005).

Early detection means a child can be identified and diagnosed with autism spectrum disorder or developmental disability and begin treatment at an early age. Early detection and treatment provides a better opportunity for children to advance in skill development. Early intervention programs are common in most states and provide children with appropriate treatment to make advancement in their developmental delays. AutPlay Therapy supports early detection of ASD. AutPlay Therapy intake and assessment processes can provide autism screenings that are useful for parents to begin to identify an ASD and subsequently refer the family to an early intervention program.

Within the AutPlay Therapy parameters, practitioners have the ability to implement autism screenings. AutPlay autism screenings serve as a tool for practitioners to observe and assess a child to identify if there appears to be a need for further evaluation or referral regarding a possible ASD. Autism screenings are not a diagnostic process; they provide a more simple procedure to screen for the need for further evaluation. Although there are many options open to a practitioner when conducting an autism screening, the following highlights the screening process in AutPlay Therapy:

1. The entire process should take 2–3 hours, which can be implanted in one setting or across session.
2. Parents are given three inventories to complete on their child. Parents can also give the inventories to other adults who know the child well so multiple individuals can complete the inventories assessing the child.
3. The three standard inventories used during the screening process are the Autism Treatment Evaluation Checklist (ATEC), the AutPlay Autism Checklist, and the Modified Checklist for Autism in Toddlers, Revised with Follow-Up (M-CHAT-R/F). These three inventories are given to parents to complete and return to the practitioner for scoring and review.
4. The practitioner will conduct an observation with the child in a playroom. This observation typically lasts 30–45 minutes. The practitioner can use the AutPlay Child Observation form located in the Appendix. The practitioner then conducts an observation of the parent and child together in a playroom. This observation lasts approximately 30 minutes. The practitioner can use the AutPlay Child/Parent Observation form located in the Appendix.
5. Once the inventories and observations have been completed, the practitioner and parent discuss the process and the results to identify if there is a need for further evaluation. If there are any significant concerns, the practitioner should refer the family to an early intervention program or for a full psychological evaluation.

Early Characteristics of Autism Spectrum Disorder

According to the National Institute of Mental Health (2015), the following are possible early childhood indicators of autism spectrum disorder:

- Child does not babble, point, or make meaningful gestures by 1 year of age.
- Child does not speak one word by 16 months old.
- Child does not combine two words by 2 years old.
- Child does not respond to his or her name.
- Child loses language or social skills.
- Child does not seem to know how to play with toys.
- Child excessively lines up toys or other objects.
- Child is attached to one particular toy or object.
- Child does not smile.

- Child, at times, seems to be hearing impaired.
- Child displays poor eye contact.

Further signs include when the child does not crawl, cannot stand when supported, does not learn to use gestures like shaking head or waving, and does not search for objects hidden while he or she watches.

Other Characteristics of Autism Spectrum Disorder

- Child does not respond to other people appropriately.
- Child ignores other children.
- Child does not make eye contact and wants to be alone.
- Child shows no interest in make believe or pretend play.
- Child speaks unclearly or in own world.
- Child loses skills he or she once displayed.
- Child does not show a wide range of emotions.
- Child has trouble understanding other people's feelings.
- Child has difficulty talking about his or her own feelings.
- Child shows behavioral extremes (unusually aggressive, fearful, sad, shy).
- Child repeats actions over and over again.
- Child has a difficult time adjusting when a routine is changed.
- Child is unusually withdrawn and not active in social situations.
- Child is easily distracted and has trouble focusing on an activity.
- Child does not respond to people or responds only superficially.
- Child cannot tell the difference between real and make believe.
- Child does not participate in a wide variety of games and activities.
- Child does not use language properly or accurately.
- Child has narrow or obsessive interests.
- Child will talk only about him- or herself or his or her own interests.
- Child speaks in an unusual way or tone of voice.
- Child has a hard time understanding body language.

Common Terms Related to Autism Spectrum Disorder

Here are common terms and definitions adapted from The National Institute of Mental Health (2015) and Autism Speaks (2015):

> **Stimming** is a repetitive body movement, such as hand flapping, which is hypothesized to stimulate one or more senses. The term is shorthand for "self-stimulation." Repetitive movement, or stereotypy, is often referred to as stimming under the hypothesis that it has a function related to sensory input.
>
> **Echolalia** is a child's automatic repetition of vocalizations made by another person. It is closely related to echopraxia, the automatic repetition of movements made by another person. Echolalia can be present with autism and other developmental disabilities. A typical pediatric presentation of

echolalia might be as follows: A child is asked, "Do you want dinner?"; the child echoes back, "Do you want dinner?" followed by a pause and then a response, "Yes. What's for dinner?" In delayed echolalia, a phrase is repeated after a delay, such as a person with autism who repeats TV commercials, favorite movie scripts, or parental reprimands.

Emotional regulation is a child's ability to notice and respond to internal and external sensory input and then adjust his emotions and behavior to the demands of his surroundings.

Receptive language is the comprehension of language—listening and understanding what is communicated. It is the receiving aspect of language. Sometimes, reading is included when referring to receptive language, but some use the term for spoken communication only. It involves being attentive to what is said, the ability to comprehend the message, the speed of processing the message, and concentrating on the message. Receptive language also includes understanding figurative language, as well as literal language. Receptive language includes being able to follow a series of commands.

Expressive language is the use of verbal behavior, or speech, to communicate thoughts, ideas, and feelings with others.

Pragmatic speech is language used to communicate and socialize.

Compulsions are deliberate repetitive behaviors that follow specific rules, such as pertaining to cleaning, checking, or counting. In young children, restricted patterns of interest may be an early sign of compulsions.

Obsessions are the domination of one's thoughts or feelings by a persistent idea, image, desire, etc. Obsessions are thoughts that recur and persist despite efforts to ignore or confront them.

Hyperarousal is a state of increased psychological and physiological tension marked by such effects as reduced pain tolerance, anxiety, exaggerated startle responses, insomnia, and fatigue.

Hypoarousal is a physiological state where the body slows down. It may include feelings of sadness, irritability, and nervousness.

Sensory processing refers to the way the nervous system receives messages from the senses and turns them into appropriate motor and behavioral responses. Processing issues exist when sensory signals do not get organized into appropriate responses, which create challenges in performing everyday tasks and may manifest in motor clumsiness, behavioral problems, anxiety, depression, and school failure. The seven sensory areas are sight, smell, taste, hearing, touch, vestibular, and proprioception.

Perseveration refers to repeating or "getting stuck" carrying out a behavior (e.g., putting in and taking out a puzzle piece) when it is no longer appropriate.

Eye gaze is looking at the face of others to check and see what they are looking at and to signal interest in interacting. It is a nonverbal behavior used to convey or exchange information or express emotions without the use of words.

Theory of mind (ToM) is the ability to attribute mental states (beliefs, intents, desires, pretending, knowledge) to oneself and others and to understand that others have beliefs, desires, and intentions that are different from one's own.

Joint attention is the shared focus of two individuals on an object. It is achieved when one individual alerts another to an object by means of eye-gazing, pointing, or some other verbal or nonverbal indication. An individual gazes at another individual, points to an object, and then returns their gaze to the individual.

Social reciprocity is the back-and-forth flow of social interaction. The term reciprocity refers to how the behavior of one person influences and is influenced by the behavior of another person, and vice versa.

Atypical is not typical or not conforming to the common type; irregular or abnormal.

Neurotypical is a label for people who are not on the autism spectrum; specifically, neurotypical people have neurological development and states that are consistent with what most people would perceive as normal.

Developmental delay is when a child does not reach his or her developmental milestones at the expected times. It is an ongoing major or minor delay in the process of development.

Spectrum disorder is a term that refers to three disorders that, using DSM-IV criteria, previously fell under the umbrella of autism spectrum disorders: autism, Asperger's syndrome, and pervasive developmental disorder, not otherwise specified.

Hyperlexia is characterized by having an average or above-average IQ and a word-reading ability well above what would be expected at a given age. It can be viewed as a super-ability in which word recognition ability goes far above expected levels of skill.

Dysregulation is a term used in the mental health community to refer to an emotional response that is poorly modulated and does not fall within the conventionally accepted range of emotive response. It can be looked at as a child's inability to manage or regulate his or her emotions, which typically results in various negative behaviors.

Individualized Education Program (IEP) is an educational plan designed to meet the unique education needs of one child, who may have a disability, as defined by federal regulations. An IEP is intended to help children reach targeted educational goals. IEPs are mandated by the Individuals with Disabilities Education Act (IDEA).

Causes of Autism Spectrum Disorder

There is no known cause for autism spectrum disorder. It is likely there are multiple causes of ASD. For a time, it was thought that poor parenting (parenting skills and approaches implemented by the mother) caused ASD. We now know this is not true. There are multiple theories about the cause of

ASD, some existing to a detrimental degree (such as poor parenting). Currently, theories for causes of ASD fall into two broad categories: genetic and environmental.

In the scientific community, autism spectrum disorder is typically thought to be a genetic disorder with multiple chromosomes and genes being impacted (National Institute of Neurological Disorders and Stroke, 2015). Some of the more common environmental thoughts on possible causes include certain foods, infectious disease, heavy metals, solvents, diesel exhaust, PCBs, phthalates, and phenols used in plastic products, pesticides, brominated flame retardants, alcohol, smoking, illicit drugs, and vaccines.

Genetics and environment may both play a role in the cause of autism spectrum disorder. A predominant belief asserts that there may be many causes and that several are a combination of both genetic and environmental factors. Although there are many thoughts and theories about what causes ASD, all thoughts and theories to date lack supporting evidence to be considered a cause.

Treatment Approaches for Autism Spectrum Disorder

There is no treatment that cures ASD, but many do help children and adolescents make great improvements. There are hundreds of reported ASD treatments, but generally, they all fall under one of four types: educational, behavioral, psychological, and biomedical (Barboa & Obrey, 2014). Not all proposed treatments fall under one of these categories, as there are many advertised alternative and holistic treatments available. The myriad of options can become overwhelming for parents who are seeking the best treatment for their child. Practitioners can assist parents by helping them understand how to categorize treatments and how to scrutinize treatments when deciding what to pursue. Exkorn (2005) proposed several questions that should be asked when evaluating a potential ASD treatment:

1. What is this treatment, and what does it do?
2. What is the intensity of the treatment?
3. Is there any real science to support this treatment?
4. Will this treatment complement the rest of my child's treatments?
5. How am I involved in supporting my child's treatment?
6. How will my child's progress be measured?
7. What is the cost of the treatment?

The majority of ASD treatments in the promising/emerging and evidence-based categories are behavioral/psychological/educational based. Many specific ASD treatments have some overlap in terms of their processes and may fall under two or all three of these categories. Most treatments that fall into one of these three categories will have a skill-based element, meaning that there is a specific goal to help increase the skill development of children and adolescents with ASD and that treatment protocol will be directed to that end. It is not uncommon for children with ASD to be involved in multiple treatments. ASD is a complex disorder, and it typically affects the child in multiple areas and having a comprehensive treatment approach where several specialized professionals can work together and each address the multiple affected areas is not only common but often recommended. Practitioners may find that they are working collaboratively with other professionals such as a speech therapist or occupational therapist and may even find they are referring the children they are working with for these additional treatments.

AutPlay Therapy combines elements of educational, behavioral, and psychological processes and has a skill development focus. Further, the foundational contributions to AutPlay are behavioral and psychological theories and treatments that have a strong evidence base in terms of being effective for children and adolescents with ASD. AutPlay Therapy, by design, is a complementary approach that can be included with other ASD treatments and the protocols of AutPlay align well with most other behavioral-, psychological-, and educational-based treatments.

What to Expect from Children with Autism Spectrum Disorder

- Child will likely have poor social skills and high levels of discomfort in social situations regardless of his or her level of functioning.
- Child will likely modulate his or her emotions poorly.
- Child will struggle with anxiety and high levels of dysregulation. Anxiety is typically the most challenging negative emotion for the child with ASD.
- Child is usually experiencing some level of dysregulation, but the question is "how much?" Many things can create dysregulation including poor regulation ability, a lack of social skills, new or unexpected situations, and sensory issues.
- Child will produce most unwanted behavior episodes when feeling dysregulated, which is typically not premeditated or controlled by the child and is often a very frightening experience for the child.
- Child will have problems handling transitions, changes to his or her schedule or routine, and new people or experiences. Any spontaneous happening will likely produce anxiety and discomfort.
- Child may appear more capable or less capable than he or she actually is.
- Child may have small and large motor and coordination challenges.
- Child may be experiencing a great deal of sensory processing issues in one or multiple areas regarding the seven senses. Sensory struggles can be challenging to identify and may involve environmental issues that seem benign to the practitioner.
- Child will likely be a visual learner and prefer to have information presented in a visual format.
- Child will usually be a concrete and literal thinker. He she will likely not do well with abstract or subjective thoughts and processes or information presented in this way.

- Child will most likely struggle verbally to communicate what he or she is thinking or feeling especially when he or she is in a dysregulated state.
- Child will most likely have challenges in receptive language ability even when his or her expressive language ability is high.
- Child will likely be inconsistent in terms of skill ability presentation. He or she may accomplish something one day that seems very challenging and, the next day, is unable to accomplish something that seems much less difficult.
- Child may present with a great deal of hyperarousal or be the exact opposite and present with a great deal of hypoarousal.
- Child may be susceptible to being bullied at school and in peer situations.
- Child may be slow to respond to questions or tasks. He or she may need extra time to process what has been said or asked of him or her.
- Child will likely experience school as the most demanding and dysregulating environment in which he or she participates.

Developmental Disabilities

Several terms are often used when discussing conditions that affect development. Developmental disorders, neurodevelopmental disorders, and developmental disabilities are three of the most common, and for the purposes of this handbook, these three terms will be used interchangeably. While autism spectrum disorder is in the category of developmental disabilities, there are several other disorders also considered developmental disabilities. According to the Centers for Disease Control and Prevention (2015), developmental disabilities are a diverse group of severe chronic conditions that are due to mental and/or physical impairments. People with developmental disabilities have problems with major life activities such as language, mobility, learning, self-help, and independent living. Developmental disabilities begin anytime during development up to 22 years of age and usually last throughout a person's lifetime.

The National Institute of Child Health and Human Development (2014) defined developmental disabilities as severe, long-term problems that may affect both physical and mental ability. The problems are usually lifelong and can impact everyday living. Often there is no cure, but treatments such as mental health counseling can help the symptoms. There are many thoughts on the causes of developmental disabilities. Evidence points to social, environmental, and physical issues that lead to developmental disabilities. Some common factors that seem to contribute to developmental disabilities include:

- Brain injuries
- Abnormalities of chromosomes and genes
- Premature births
- Problems during pregnancy
- Drug and alcohol abuse during pregnancy
- Severe child abuse

There are many nervous system, sensory, dysregulation, and metabolic developmental disorders and disabilities that exist. Complete definitions of all developmental disorders are not presented in this handbook, but many developmental disorders have been treated with AutPlay Therapy, including attention deficit hyperactivity disorder (ADHD), Down syndrome, fragile X syndrome, sensory integration disorders, cerebral palsy, expressive language disorder, seizure disorders, Tourette's syndrome, learning disorders, and various chromosome disorders. The following is a brief introduction to some of the more common developmental disorders that have been divided by diagnosis classification (medical, occupational, and psychological):

Medical

Down syndrome: Down syndrome is a condition in which a person is born with an extra copy of chromosome 21. People with Down syndrome can have physical problems as well as intellectual disabilities. Delayed development and behavioral problems are often reported in children with Down syndrome. Affected individuals' speech and language develop later and more slowly than in children without Down syndrome, and affected individuals' speech may be more difficult to understand. Behavioral issues can include attention problems, obsessive/compulsive behavior, and stubbornness or tantrums. A small percentage of people with Down syndrome are also diagnosed with autism spectrum disorder, which affects communication and social interaction (National Institute of Neurological Disorders and Stroke, 2015).

Fragile X syndrome: Mutations in the FMR1 gene cause fragile X syndrome. Fragile X syndrome is a genetic condition that causes a range of developmental problems including learning disabilities and cognitive impairment. Usually, males are more severely affected by this disorder than females.

   Affected individuals usually have delayed development of speech and language by age 2. Most males with fragile X syndrome have mild to moderate intellectual disability, while about one-third of affected females are intellectually disabled. Children with fragile X syndrome may also have anxiety and hyperactive behavior such as fidgeting or impulsive actions. They may have attention deficit disorder (ADD), which includes an impaired ability to maintain attention and difficulty focusing on specific tasks. About one-third of individuals with fragile X syndrome have features of autism spectrum disorder that affect communication and social interaction. Seizures occur in about 15 percent of males and approximately 5 percent of females with fragile X syndrome (National Institute of Neurological Disorders and Stroke, 2015).

Cerebral palsy: The term *cerebral palsy* refers to any one of a number of neurological disorders that appear in infancy or early childhood and permanently affect body movement and muscle coordination but don't worsen over time. Even though cerebral palsy affects muscle movement, it isn't caused by problems in the muscles or nerves. It is caused by abnormalities in parts of the brain that control muscle movements. The majority of children with cerebral palsy are born with it, although it may not be detected until months or years later. The early signs of cerebral palsy usually appear before a child reaches 3 years of age. The most common signs are a lack of muscle coordination when performing voluntary movements (ataxia); stiff or tight muscles and exaggerated reflexes (spasticity); walking with one foot or leg dragging; walking on the toes, a crouched gait, or a "scissored" gait; and muscle tone that is either too stiff or too floppy (National Institute of Neurological Disorders and Stroke, 2015).

Seizure disorders: Seizures happen when your brain cells, which communicate through electrical signals, send out abnormal signals. Having several seizures (recurrent seizures) is considered epilepsy. Seizures are not considered epilepsy if they occur only once or are correctable. Epilepsy can happen at any age, but it is most common in the elderly. Many children with epilepsy outgrow the condition. However, even mild seizures that happen more than once should be treated because they could cause harm if they happen while you are driving, walking, or swimming, for example.

Partial seizures involve a part of the brain. They can be:

1. **Simple partial seizures:** Symptoms may include involuntary twitching of the muscles or arms and legs, changes in vision, vertigo, and experiencing unusual tastes or smells. The person does not lose consciousness.
2. **Complex partial seizures:** Symptoms may be similar to those of partial seizures, but the person does lose awareness for a time. The person may engage in repetitive behavior (like walking in a circle or rubbing their hands) or stare.

Generalized seizures involve much more or all of the brain. They can be:

1. **Absence seizures (petit mal):** Symptoms may include staring and brief loss of consciousness.
2. **Myoclonic seizures:** Symptoms may include jerking or twitching of the limbs on both sides of the body.
3. **Tonic-clonic seizures (grand mal):** Symptoms may include loss of consciousness, shaking or jerking of the body, and loss of bladder control. The person may have an aura or an unusual feeling before the seizure starts. These seizures can last from 5–20 minutes (National Institute of Neurological Disorders and Stroke, 2015).

Occupational

Sensory processing/integration disorder is a condition that exists when sensory signals do not get organized into appropriate responses. Pioneering occupational practitioner and neuroscientist A. Jean Ayres, PhD, likened sensory processing disorder (SPD) to a neurological "traffic jam" that prevents certain parts of the brain from receiving the information needed to interpret sensory information correctly. A person with SPD finds it difficult to process and act upon information received through the senses, which creates challenges in performing countless everyday tasks. Motor clumsiness, behavioral problems, anxiety, depression, school failure, and other impacts may result if the disorder is not treated effectively.

SPD can affect people in only one sense—for example, just touch or just sight or just movement—or in multiple senses. One person with SPD may over-respond to sensation and find clothing, physical contact, light, sound, food, or other sensory input to be unbearable. Another might under-respond and show little or no reaction to stimulation, even pain or extreme hot and cold. In children whose sensory processing of messages from the muscles and joints is impaired, posture and motor skills can be affected. These are the "floppy babies" who worry new parents and the kids who get called "klutz" and "spaz" on the playground. Still other children exhibit an appetite for sensation that is in perpetual overdrive (Sensory Processing Disorder Foundation, 2015).

Psychological

Intellectual developmental disorder is a disorder that includes both a current intellectual deficit and a deficit in adaptive functioning with onset during the developmental period. The following three criteria must be met:

1. Intellectual developmental disorder is characterized by deficits in general mental abilities such as reasoning, problem solving, planning, abstract thinking, judgment, academic learning, and learning from experience.
2. Impairment in adaptive functioning for the individual's age and sociocultural background, which refers to how well a person meets the standards of personal independence and social responsibility in one or more aspects of daily life activities, such as communication, social participation, functioning at school or at work, or personal independence at home or in community settings. The limitations result in the need for ongoing support at school, work, or independent life.
3. All symptoms must have an onset during the developmental period (American Psychiatric Association, dsm5.org, 2014).

Social pragmatic communication disorder (SCD) is characterized by a persistent difficulty with verbal and nonverbal communication that cannot be explained by low cognitive ability. Symptoms include difficulty in the acquisition and use of spoken and written language as well as problems with inappropriate responses in conversation. The disorder limits effective communication, social relationships, academic achievement, or occupational performance. Symptoms must be present in early childhood even if they are not recognized until later when speech, language, or communication demands exceed abilities (American Psychiatric Association, dsm5.org, 2014).

Tourette's syndrome (TS) is a neurological disorder characterized by repetitive, stereotyped, involuntary movements and vocalizations called tics. Many individuals with TS experience additional neurobehavioral problems that often cause more impairment than the tics themselves. These include inattention, hyperactivity and impulsivity (attention deficit hyperactivity disorder —ADHD); problems with reading, writing, and arithmetic; and obsessive-compulsive symptoms such as intrusive thoughts/worries and repetitive behaviors. For example, worries about dirt and germs may be associated with repetitive hand washing, and concerns about bad things happening may be associated with ritualistic behaviors such as counting, repeating, or ordering and arranging. People with TS have also reported problems with depression or anxiety disorders, as well as other difficulties with living that may or may not be directly related to TS (National Institute of Neurological Disorders and Stroke, 2015).

Attention deficit hyperactivity disorder (ADHD)—Scientists are not sure what causes ADHD, although many studies suggest that genes play a large role. Like many other illnesses, ADHD probably results from a combination of factors. In addition to genetics, researchers are looking at possible environmental factors and are studying how brain injuries, nutrition, and the social environment might contribute to ADHD. Attention deficit hyperactivity disorder is one of the most common childhood disorders and can continue through adolescence and adulthood. Symptoms include difficulty staying focused and paying attention, difficulty controlling behavior, and hyperactivity (overactivity). Inattention, hyperactivity, and impulsivity are the key behaviors of ADHD (National Institute of Mental Health, 2015).

Many developmental disabilities have no cure, but there are ways to treat the symptoms that present with developmental disabilities. AutPlay Therapy aims to help treat the symptoms that often occur with developmental disabilities. AutPlay Therapy targets emotional regulation, social functioning, relationship connection and behavior issues (all common issues seen in developmental disabilities) to increase skill acquisition in these areas for individuals with developmental disabilities (see Table 1.1). AutPlay Therapy also helps with assessing and addressing issues of independent living skills.

Table 1.1 Treatment of Developmental Disorders with AutPlay Therapy

Developmental Disorders	Primary Symptoms Addressed through AutPlay Therapy
Autism spectrum disorder, social pragmatic communication disorder, Tourette's syndrome, attention deficit hyperactivity disorder, cerebral palsy, Down syndrome, fragile X, seizure disorders, sensory processing disorder, and intellectual developmental disorder	Emotional regulation, social functioning, inattention, hyperactivity, obsessive and intrusive thoughts, repetitive behaviors, dysregulation, anxiety and worry, low self-worth, relationship connection, and skill development

Many children and adolescents with a developmental disability enter into AutPlay Therapy to gain improvement in social skills, to increase their ability to regulate their emotions, and to reduce anxiety and dysregulation issues. Practitioners working with children with a variety of developmental disabilities should educate themselves on the specifics of each disability and recognize that many of these children will be involved in other treatment interventions, both behavioral and medical. Creating a collaborative approach between all professionals working with a child with a developmental disability is most recommended.

2 Foundations of AutPlay Therapy

AutPlay Therapy Overview

AutPlay Therapy is a play therapy and behavioral therapy-based approach to working with children and adolescents with autism spectrum disorder, other neurodevelopmental disorders, and developmental disabilities. AutPlay is a mental health therapeutic treatment approach that builds upon established psychological and counseling theory as well as incorporates evidence-based behavioral approaches for addressing children and adolescents with ASD and other developmental disorders. AutPlay Therapy is a combination of behavioral and developmental methodology and treatment protocol is both practitioner and parent led. AutPlay incorporates a comprehensive approach to addressing the myriad of issues confronting children with ASD similar to several established treatment approaches such as the Early Start Denver Model (ESDM), Building Blocks, SCERTS, and TEACCH, which are described in the Appendix.

The AutPlay Therapy approach is strongly influenced by theoretical orientations of play therapy and behavioral therapy. Although AutPlay Therapy functions as a unique and comprehensive treatment model, components of various play therapy approaches and behavioral therapy methods can be identified throughout the AutPlay process. A brief presentation of the primary influences on AutPlay Therapy is presented in this handbook. Practitioners are encouraged to learn more about the influence areas that are highlighted in this handbook to heighten their own knowledge and awareness of approaches and protocols that are most beneficial in treating children and adolescents with autism spectrum disorder.

Play Therapy

The Association for Play Therapy (2015) defines play therapy as "the systematic use of a theoretical model to establish an interpersonal process wherein trained play practitioners use the therapeutic powers of play to help clients prevent or resolve psychosocial difficulties and achieve optimal growth and development."

O'Conner (2000) contended that there is a biological, intrapersonal, interpersonal, and sociocultural function of play behavior in the lives of children and furthered the definition of play therapy: Play therapy consists of a cluster of treatment modalities that involve the systematic use of a theoretical model to establish an interpersonal process. In play therapy, trained play practitioners use the therapeutic powers of play to help clients prevent or resolve psychosocial difficulties and achieve optimal growth and development and the re-establishment of the child's ability to engage in play behavior as it is classically defined.

Schaefer (2003) presented several therapeutic factors of play. He proposed that play helps in relationship enhancement, expressive communication, growth of competence, creative problem solving, abreaction, role-play, learning through metaphor, positive emotion, and socialization. Children can learn social skills, develop relationships, learn how to communicate and express themselves through verbal and nonverbal means, and develop problem-solving abilities through therapeutic play.

Play therapy can best be thought of as an umbrella term, as there are currently several play therapy theories and approaches that exist. Play therapy approaches range from being nondirective to directive in terms of the practitioner's involvement in the process with their clients. Some theories of play therapy rely heavily on the use of toys and props while other theories use toys minimally. Most play therapy approaches involve some use of toys, props, art, music, movement, or games as an avenue to help clients achieve their therapeutic goals.

Play therapy approaches hold many benefits for children and adolescents with autism spectrum disorder especially in treating social and emotional issues they typically struggle with. Play therapy is uniquely designed for and responsive to the individual and developmental needs of each child, and recently, there has been an increase in child therapy literature emphasizing play as the ideal way to treat social and emotional difficulties in children (Bratton, Ray, Rhine, & Jones, 2005; Josefi & Ryan, 2004). Research has shown that children diagnosed with ASD and participating in play therapy have gained improvement in pretend play, attachment, social interaction, self-regulation, coping with changes, emotional response, and autonomy (Josefi & Ryan, 2004).

The benefits of children engaging in play include cognitive development (learning, thinking, and planning, etc.); social skills (practicing social interaction, roles and routines); language (talking to others, turn taking, etc.); problem solving (negotiation, asking for help, solving difficulties, etc.); and emotional development (managing feelings, understanding others, empathy, etc.). Children with play skills are more likely to be included with their peers, and play is a key learning tool through which children develop social skills, flexibility, core learning skills, and language. Play also provides opportunities for children to practice events, situations, and routines in a safe place, with no pressure to "get it right" (Phillips & Beavan, 2010).

Sherratt & Peter (2002) suggested that play interventions and experiences are extremely important to children with autism spectrum disorder. They stated that simultaneously activating the areas of the brain associated with emotions and generative thought while explicitly teaching children with ASD to play will lead to success. Further, Thornton & Cox (2005) conducted individual play sessions with children with ASD specifically to address their challenging behaviors. They incorporated techniques that included relationship development, gaining attention, turn taking, enjoyment, and structure. Their research found that play interventions did impact on the child's behavior with a reduction in negative behavior following the structured play interventions.

Play Therapy and play-based treatments can be appropriate interventions in working with children with ASD especially when working with children who have little in the way of social skills and poor communication (Parker & O'Brien, 2011). Play-based interventions are gaining more and more valid research as effective treatment approaches for children and adolescents with ASD and other neurodevelopmental disorders. Play-based interventions provide the opportunity for the practitioner to individualize treatment and engage the child in a playful and natural way that other ASD treatments may not offer.

Play therapy approaches have been successfully implemented for children, adolescents, adults, families, couples, and groups. Play therapy offers the ability to communicate inner processes and emotions without using verbal communication and provides awareness properties to help put words to otherwise unidentified issues. The freedom from judgment and the ability to create and explore through play therapy offers safety for clients and facilitates an almost innate desire that exists in all people—the desire to play.

Arguably, many play therapy theories and approaches have had some effect or influence on the creation of AutPlay Therapy, but the play therapy approaches that have been the most influential on AutPlay Therapy include Theraplay, filial therapy, family play therapy, and cognitive behavioral play therapy. Although play therapy as a whole is the base for AutPlay Therapy, these approaches have specific elements and constructs that have more directly impacted the work of AutPlay Therapy. The following presents a further review of the four play therapy approaches most influential upon AutPlay Therapy.

The play therapy approaches of Theraplay, filial therapy, and family play therapy all provide a comprehensive treatment approach to working with children and parents in a family play therapy approach designed to create healthy relationship connection, problem solving, behavior modification, and to some degree skill development. These play therapy approaches focus on the ability of a child to develop healthy and lasting relationships, with the primary focus of relationship development being the relationship between child and parent. Through this process, other issues such as reducing unwanted behaviors and improving skill development can also be mastered. Cognitive behavioral play therapy (CBPT) incorporates cognitive therapy methodology with play-based activities to help children understand and regulate emotions, change behaviors, and gain new skills. It is a directive approach that provides education, role modeling, and practice by utilizing play, which helps children to stay involved in treatment due to the more fun and relaxed process that the play creates.

Theraplay

Theraplay is a playful, engaging, short-term treatment method that is intimate, physical, personal, focused, and fun. It is modeled on the natural, healthy parent-infant relationship, and treatment actively involves parents. The focus of Theraplay treatment is on the underlying disturbances in the relationship between the child and his or her caretakers. The goal of treatment is to enhance attachment, self-esteem, trust, and joyful engagement and to empower parents to continue on their own healthy interaction with their child (Jernberg & Booth, 2001).

Booth & Jernberg (2010) reported that there are four dimensions that are used in treatment planning to meet the needs of the child and the parent in treatment. The four Theraplay dimensions are structure, engagement, nurture, and challenge. The following is a brief explanation of each dimension:

> **Structure:** Parents are trustworthy and provide safety and regulation.
> **Engagement:** Parents provide playful experiences that create a strong connection.
> **Nurture:** Parents respond empathically and provide a safe haven for the child.
> **Challenge:** Parents encourage the child to strive, take risks, and explore.

A practitioner trained in Theraplay protocol works with the child and parents in a family play therapy context to help work on improvement and success in each of the four dimensions. Practitioners typically meet with the child and parent together to model and implement play interventions designed to meet treatment goals. The overall goal of treatment is to establish a trusting emotional relationship between the child and his or her parents.

AutPlay Therapy is influenced by Theraplay in that relationship development (connection) is achieved by parent and child in process together to create engagement and connection through natural, fun, play-based techniques. It is important to note that Theraplay is an established treatment option that has had a great deal of success in treating children with ASD. Jernberg & Booth (2001) have proposed that Theraplay is particularly helpful in the treatment of children with autism disorders because it does not depend on their being able to respond to language. Further, Theraplay concentrates on the precursors to cognition and to representational thinking, mutual attention, and engagement, making it an ideal treatment for children with relationship and communication difficulties.

Bundy-Myrow (2012) stated the following in regard to the benefits of treating children with autism spectrum disorder using Theraplay:

> What differentiates Theraplay for children with Autism Spectrum Disorder from other play therapy approaches is twofold: As the primary playroom object, the Theraplay practitioner uses sensorimotor-based play to engage the child and counter autistic patterns. To empower parents as

therapeutic partners, the Theraplay practitioner demonstrates and guides parents to provide the unique relationship building blocks their child needs for development.

Booth & Jernberg (2010) stated that Theraplay is ideally suited for children with ASD because Theraplay treatment engages children in a playful, positive social interaction that focuses on establishing the basis of the capacity to engage with others and participate in relationships. Simeone-Russell (2011) furthered that the use of group Theraplay has been found to be very effective in developing engagement, interaction, communication, language, and social skills in children with autism spectrum disorder. In working with children with ASD, typical goals of Theraplay include increasing eye contact, increasing attention and turn taking, adjusting to transitions and changes, helping parents to discover methods to calm and soothe their child, and stimulating communication.

AutPlay Therapy and Theraplay share some similar characteristics. Both include the parent in the treatment process and emphasize the role of the parent as a partner or co-change agent along with the practitioner. Both involve the treatment protocol of teaching parents how to interact or work on skill development through directive play-based interventions. And both work on relationship development or connection and skill development simultaneously using play therapy as the main catalyst to reach treatment goals.

Filial Therapy

Filial therapy is a theoretically integrative psychoeducational model of therapy in which parents serve as the primary change agents for their children. In essence, it is a form of family therapy that uses play therapy methods to enhance parent-child relationships and to solve a wide range of child and family problems (VanFleet, 2012). In filial therapy, the practitioner teaches parents how to have child-centered play therapy sessions at home. The parent learns the principles and conducts the play times with their child in the home setting.

Guerney (2003) stated that the basic model or goals of filial therapy include reducing problem behaviors in the child, enhancing the parent-child relationship, optimizing child adjustment and increasing child competence and self-confidence, and improving parenting skills. These goals are attained by including parents in the process and empowering them to become change agents in working with their child. The overall goal of filial therapy is to focus on improvement in the parent-child relationship and subsequently produce improvement in other areas as well.

VanFleet (2014) furthered that filial therapy comprises eight essential features. These features can be found individually or in smaller combinations in other interventions, but it is the presence of all eight that defines filial therapy.

1. The importance of play in child development is highlighted, and play is seen as the primary avenue for gaining greater understanding of children.

2. Parents are empowered as the change agents for their own children.
3. The client is the relationship, not the individual.
4. Empathy is essential for growth and change.
5. The entire family is involved whenever possible.
6. A psychoeducational training model is used with parents.
7. Tangible support and continued learning are provided through live supervision of parents early play sessions with their children.
8. The process is truly collaborative.

VanFleet (1994) stated that the overall aim of filial therapy is to eliminate the presenting problems at their source; develop positive interactions between parents and their children; and increase families' communication, coping, and problem-solving skills so they are better able to handle future problems independently and successfully. VanFleet (2014) furthered that filial therapy offers several potential benefits to families of children with an autism spectrum disorder. The filial therapy process provides children with ASD safety and choices without pressure, and there is no need for verbal communication ability as communication can be done through play. Perhaps the greatest value is the empowerment of parents, giving them tools with which to better understand and communicate with their children.

Filial therapy's influence on AutPlay Therapy is evident in methods that incorporate a parent-training approach where the parents are taught AutPlay techniques to do at home with their child. In both approaches, parents are taught to become co-change agents for their child. Relationship connection and parent empowerment are both central features of filial therapy and AutPlay Therapy. The AutPlay Follow Me Approach in particular highlights several foundations of filial therapy including filial play skills such as tracking, reflecting, letting the child lead, teaching parents to have Follow Me play times at home with their child, and focusing on relationship development and connection.

Family Play Therapy

Family play therapy involves the parents and child together in therapy sessions. Play therapy techniques become a part of the therapeutic family process and are utilized to help engage all members of the family and to help reach treatment goals. Gil (1994) stated that the practitioner can teach parents to observe, decode, and participate in their child's play in such a way that their understanding of their child's experience is enhanced and the possibility for deeper emotional contact with their child becomes available.

Gil (2003) stated that, in family play therapy, family members are seen together as a system to achieve systemic changes. The application of play therapy and verbal therapy approaches are used. The practitioner implements a variety of play therapy tasks and invites participation in the tasks from all family members. Play therapy tasks are designed to assess and understand underlying issues and promote positive change within the family system. There is not one identified client; the whole family is the client. The family play practitioner will likely have several directive play therapy interventions in his or her "toolbox" to implement with a family to address specific issues happening within that family with the purpose of addressing and reaching established treatment goals.

Family play therapy's influence on AutPlay Therapy involves the understanding that a parent's interaction with their child through play methods can have a deep and purposeful impact on their child and on the entire family system. AutPlay Therapy at its basic is a family play therapy approach. The family system is arguably never more evident than in a family who has a child with autism spectrum disorder or any other developmental disorder. The family unit as a whole is often effected by and engaged with the various issues and components of having a child with special needs. This realization makes treatment approaches with a family focus necessary and relevant. Most established ASD treatments believe that treatment should focus on the whole family and actively incorporate the parents and/or other family members in the process due to the understanding that the whole family system is impacted by ASD.

Relationship development approaches, especially those grounded in play therapy methods, heavily influence the AutPlay Therapy component area of connection and transcend throughout the AutPlay Therapy approach, which emphasizes the importance of parent involvement and the important role that parents have in the AutPlay Therapy process. AutPlay Therapy functions as a family play therapy approach in that parents and/or other family members are actively involved in the treatment approach, engaging in and learning directive play therapy interventions to improve relationship connection and skill development.

Cognitive Behavioral Play Therapy (CBPT)

Susan M. Knell (2004) conceptualized cognitive behavioral play therapy (CBPT) as a treatment approach that incorporates cognitive and behavioral interventions within a play therapy paradigm. Play activities as well as verbal and nonverbal forms of communication are used in resolving problems. Knell defines six specific properties related to CBPT:

1. CBPT involves the child in treatment via play.
2. CBPT focuses on the child's thoughts, feelings, fantasies, and environment.
3. CBPT provides a strategy or strategies for developing more adaptive thoughts and behaviors.
4. CBPT is structured, directive, and goal oriented rather than open ended.
5. CBPT incorporates empirically demonstrated techniques.
6. CBPT allows for an empirical examination of treatment.

In cognitive behavioral play therapy, the practitioner can present developmentally appropriate interventions that help the child master CBT methodology.

A wide array of cognitive and behavioral interventions can be incorporated into play therapy to address a wide array of issues (Drewes, 2009). CBPT interventions provide an opportunity for children to understand how their thoughts affect their behaviors and ways to change thoughts and behaviors. CBPT's emphasis on doing, rather than talking, allows children to practice all the new skills they have learned and to generalize them to their lives outside of the play therapy session.

Drewes (2009) stated that CBPT provides a wonderful opportunity to help children decrease anxiety (a common struggle emotion for children with ASD) by incorporating play activities as a vehicle to involvement and exposure it may help a child to manage and decrease anxiety and experience treatment in a more positive and fun atmosphere. Further, CBPT can be beneficial in helping children who experience emotional dysregulation. Children who experience emotional dysregulation (as many children with ASD experience) can have sudden explosions of out-of-control behavior, high levels of anxiety, and difficulties with concentration and focus. Through various cognitive methods paired with play activities, children with these issues gain a greater mastery of their emotions and thus experience less of the issues created by dysregulation.

The use of play to teach skills or alternative behaviors is a common aspect of CBPT. Educating the child takes place in the CBPT model; for example, a puppet behaves in such a way that teaches the child to express emotions or gain a new skill. Through CBPT, children can address their feelings and issues and learn more adaptive ways of dealing with their feelings. Initially, this could involve nonverbal expression and verbal labeling that is modeled for the child by the practitioner. Later, if the child begins to talk to the practitioner, more direct verbal labeling of feelings or addressing of issues can be explored (Knell, 2004).

Cognitive behavioral play therapy provides several influences on AutPlay Therapy. First, the approach of having a specific agenda for each session where specific techniques are taught is a predominant component of AutPlay Therapy. Second, the goal of helping clients understand a connection between their thinking and behaviors, and making changes in behavior is an important goal of AutPlay Therapy. Third, incorporating homework assignments and practice for repetition to acquire mastery is a highlighted component of AutPlay Therapy. Finally, the suggestion that various cognitive and behavioral play-based interventions can be taught to children to help them gain mastery, and modify their behaviors through a play-based approach is a view that is shared in AutPlay Therapy.

Behavioral Therapy

Behavioral therapy is focused on helping an individual understand how changing their behavior can lead to changes in how they are feeling. The goal of behavioral therapy is usually focused on increasing the person's engagement in positive or socially reinforcing activities. Behavioral therapy is a structured approach that carefully measures what the person is doing and then seeks to increase chances for positive experience. Some common techniques include self-monitoring, creating a daily or weekly schedule of activities, role-playing, and behavior modification approaches (PsychCentral, 2014).

The Association for Behavioral and Cognitive Therapies (2014) provided the following on behavioral therapy:

> Behavioral approaches vary; however, they focus mostly on how some thoughts or behaviors may accidentally get "rewarded" within one's environment, contributing to an increase in the frequency of these thoughts and behaviors. Behavior therapies can be applied to a wide range of psychological symptoms to adults, adolescents, and children. Although behavioral therapies are different from disorder to disorder, a common thread is that behavioral practitioners encourage clients to try new behaviors and not to allow negative "rewards" to dictate the ways in which they act.

An example:

> Imagine being a child afraid of toilets. To avoid the fear and anxiety, you might eventually choose to avoid all bathrooms and begin to have accidents in your clothes. The act of going to the bathroom in your clothes could cause you physical issues, social problems, and even affect self-worth. However, despite these consequences, the fear that comes with being around a toilet is too great to bear. Behavior practitioners suggest that avoiding the toilet has been rewarded with the absence of anxiety and fear. Behavioral treatments would involve supervised and guided experience with using a toilet until the "rewards" associated with avoidance have been "un-learned" and the negative associations you have with toilets have been "un-learned."

Two important variables in understanding behavioral therapy are stimuli (antecedent environmental events and consequences to behavior) and responses (behavior). A stimulus is something in the environment that is observable. A stimulus can be simple such as the color of an object or more complex such as what a best friend is doing and saying. Behavior is an action that is observable. A child might be covertly thinking, but there is an observable action (Williams & Williams, 2011). In behavioral therapy, when approaching any behavior, there are three important questions to ask, "What immediately precedes the behavior?" "What precisely is the behavior?" and "What immediately follows the behavior?" These are the ABCs: the antecedent, the behavior, and the consequence (Coplan, 2010).

Child-focused behavioral therapy provides a potentially powerful arena for children to change their own behavior. The variety of direct behavioral interventions with young children has expanded greatly since its inception. With young children, the treatments often involve the simple application of a behavioral procedure within a play therapy setting; behavioral techniques are used within the context of play. Most behavioral interventions with children have focused on two treatment options or the combination of the two: treating the child via the parent and direct work with the child (Knell, 2004). Behavioral interventions for children and adolescents might involve role-playing through a situation to decrease anxiety or teaching an appropriate response in regard to a situation, prompting and reinforcement activities or rewards to increase a wanted behavior, or creating a daily visual schedule to help with regulation and anxiety reduction.

Arguably, the most common and evidence-based treatment approaches for children and adolescents with autism spectrum disorder or other developmental disorders are behavioral-based treatments. Behavioral therapy, behavior modification approaches, applied behavioral analysis, cognitive behavioral therapy, and a myriad of other behavior-based therapies and treatments have been shown to be successful in improving a variety of issues that children with ASD tend to struggle with. Most early intervention programs and special education classrooms are based on some type of behavioral approach or theory. Behavioral therapy-based and expanded approaches have been used to successfully treat thousands of children with autism spectrum disorder (Coplan, 2010).

Behavioral therapy's influence on AutPlay Therapy is evident in many aspects. AutPlay Therapy attends to the child's behaviors with a goal of changing the behavior through directive interventions that are both practitioner and parent led. These interventions are play based and have the ultimate goal of helping children and adolescents with ASD to increase their skill ability. AutPlay Therapy also attends to what is occurring in the child's environment that may be creating unwanted behaviors. Further, several play-based interventions designed to increase skill development mimic behavioral therapy components such as exposure, role-playing, modeling, and shaping. AutPlay Therapy is influenced by both behavior methods and relational methods as opposed to addressing only one of these aspects. In this way, AutPlay Therapy functions as a comprehensive or holistic approach to help meet the totality of needs expressed by the child with ASD.

3 The AutPlay Therapy Approach

AutPlay Therapy Overview

AutPlay Therapy is a play therapy and behavioral therapy treatment approach for working with children and adolescents with autism spectrum disorder, developmental disabilities, or other neurodevelopmental disorders. The foundation of AutPlay Therapy consists of play therapy approaches combined with behavioral therapy approaches. As a comprehensive model, AutPlay Therapy is designed to assist children and adolescents in gaining needed skills and abilities and to teach parents how to assist their children in gaining skills and abilities.

AutPlay Therapy is a combination approach of both developmental and behavioral methodology. AutPlay Therapy addresses and assesses the developmental issues for children and adolescents and provides continuous awareness of developmental levels, deficits, and progress. At the same time, AutPlay Therapy takes into consideration and addresses the behavioral elements that children and adolescents are facing and establishes directive play therapy techniques that are both practitioner and parent led to help improve behavior.

AutPlay Therapy incorporates a combination of directive play techniques with behavioral and play therapy approaches to teach children development in three primary target areas: emotional regulation, social functioning, and connection. AutPlay protocol also addresses three secondary target areas: sensory processing, anxiety reduction, and behavioral change. When children can learn to self-regulate, possess social skills that relate to the environments they are asked to function in, and learn appropriate and meaningful relationship connection, they are less likely to have behavioral issues and more likely to function successfully in their day-to-day environment.

Children and adolescents with autism spectrum disorder or other developmental disorders often struggle with emotional regulation, social skills, and relationship connection. There tends to be a relationship among these component areas in regard to deficits and improvements. (If a child has deficits in one area, he or she will likely have deficits in the other areas; if a child improves in one area, he or she will likely improve in the other areas.) For example, as a child's emotional regulation ability improves, it will have a positive effect on his or her social skills. As a child's social skills improve, it will have a positive effect on his or her ability to connect with others.

AutPlay Therapy incorporates a parent-training component where parents are trained in using various play therapy techniques at home with their child. Parents are empowered to become co-change agents in helping their child develop and advance in skill level. AutPlay Therapy's parent-training component teaches parents how to conduct AutPlay techniques at home. Parents learn procedures and techniques and are shown how to implement techniques at home to increase specific skill and ability levels in their child.

Arguably, AutPlay Therapy functions as a family play therapy approach involving both the child and the parent in the therapeutic process. Using a play therapy base that is a natural language for the child enables the parent to be involved with their child in a way that teaches skills and increases abilities within a fun and connecting process. Further, when possible and appropriate, AutPlay Therapy involves the whole family including siblings and extended family members in the treatment process.

AutPlay Therapy relies heavily on play-based interventions and techniques to help attain skill development. Given that play is a significant focus of Aut-Play Therapy, it is important to examine what play generally looks like for a child with autism spectrum disorder. What are the similarities and differences from a neurotypical child? What can a practitioner expect a client's play to look like when beginning the AutPlay Therapy process? Table 3.1 provides an overview of neurotypical versus atypical play in children age's birth through 10 years.

In general, children with ASD lack spontaneous, flexible, imaginative, and social qualities that are common with play. Playing with toys spontaneously, engaging in pretend and imaginative play, understanding metaphor in play, and successfully engaging in group play are not likely. Children with ASD are more likely to manipulate objects in a detached fashion rather than play either functionally or symbolically. Cross (2010) listed five common play challenges that limit a child or adolescent with ASD's play potential and developmental skill acquisition:

1. Repetitious play
2. Continual roaming around the playroom
3. Continual anxiousness about or during play
4. Continual detachment or unfriendliness during play
5. Continual rejection by playmates during play

When a child with autism spectrum disorder enters a playroom or any play environment, it is likely that he or she will not engage in play in traditional or socially deemed "correct" ways to play. A child with ASD might be very hesitant at first, taking a long time to get comfortable or familiar with what is around him or her and then eventually engaging in some way; other children may isolate themselves and play with toys in a functional way, paying no attention to other people or things around them; some children may find an

Table 3.1 Neurotypical vs. Atypical Play in Children (Birth–10 Years)

Age	Neurotypical Play Development	Atypical Play Development
0–24 months	A child explores the world through the senses by mouthing objects, listening to sounds, looking at mobiles, etc.	Child does not explore and does not appear to notice, listen, or look at things. No shared cooing or smiling.
10 months	Social reciprocal interaction begins, especially with parents, such as playing peek-a-boo.	Child does not interact, make eye contact, or engage in any basic interacting games.
1–2 years	Imitates adults, then may imitate other children. May imitate mommy talking on the phone. Functional play emerges. Playing with a toy as it is intended to be played with, such as stacking blocks, rolling a car on a surface, etc.	Child does not speak, does not have joint attention, and does not play with toys as they are supposed to be played with. Odd or no play. Does not play games with caregivers.

2–3 years	Parallel play (playing side-by-side with a peer) emerges. Having the intention to be in proximity to peers during play.
	
	    Child may play beside a familiar peer in a sandbox. This starts with minimal verbal interaction with peers and gradually increases to watching and imitating peers, showing and commenting to peers, etc.
	
	    Symbolic play emerges. Pretending with toys that look like real-life objects, like flying a toy airplane through the sky, pretending to cook with a pan on a play stove, pretending to eat play food, making people or animal figurines walk and talk.
		Does not play with peers or show any interest in playing with peers and may not notice other peers. Does not do any imitation-based play.
		
		    Does not do any pretend play. Continues to lack in playing with toys appropriately or engaging caregiver in basic play games.

(*Continued*)

Table 3.1 (Continued)

Age	Neurotypical Play Development	Atypical Play Development
3 years	Play becomes more advanced and may involve peers and others more. May build and construct play objects (train sets, building houses, constructing LEGOs, making things out of play dough such as flowers, houses, faces, etc.). Child will engage in parallel play, functional, and symbolic play often with other children but still may have difficulty with sharing and cooperative play. Role-play and enactment emerges. Pretending to be in familiar roles (such as a teacher, doctor, bus driver, etc.).	Continues to not play with peers or show any interest in playing with peers. If playing with toys, may play with same toys over and over or line toys up continually. Does not do any symbolic play or role-playing. Need for routine and predictability.
4 years	Role-play and symbolic play become more and more advanced, and children begin to learn how to play cooperatively. Pretend roles now may involve peers and still tend to be related to roles they have witnessed whether in person, on TV, or in a book. Theory of mind emerges, the ability to consider that others have different thoughts, feelings, and knowledge than I do. Things can be other than what they seem. Coincides with development of more abstract play such as pretending a pencil is an airplane flying through the sky. Negotiation skills emerge as there is more awareness of others' desires and differences in thinking.	Child continues to lack symbolic and pretend play. Child continues to lack interest in playing with peers. Child will not play with peers in a cooperative fashion. Child shows no theory of mind concept. Child may focus on specific toys/items and be somewhat obsessive and rigid about the toy/item. If playing, may play with the same toy or play same scenario repeatedly.
5–6 years	Child may engage in complex play schemes with multiple other children. Involves all types of play, including cooperating and negotiating with peers to develop play schemes and carry them out.	Child's play development has not increased from early developmental levels. Child is narrow in play interests and activities. Child continues to show no interest in playing with peers.
7–10 years	Child continues to develop more imaginative play, involving things that don't actually exist.	Child displays obvious play issues regarding all previously mentioned atypical play characteristics.

object not traditionally considered a toy but manipulate and "play" with the object and ignore popular toys around them.

When children with autism spectrum disorder are given the opportunity to play freely, they are likely to pursue repetitive activities that produce the same play over and over. Some children may produce and participate in elaborate play scenarios that look like pretend play, but when examined more closely, the play is very rigid and performed repetitively with the child coming back to the same scenarios over and over again for long periods of time (Kaduson, 2008). Often children with ASD will enter a play scenario and begin playing in a way that very much looks like symbolic or pretend play. Children will manipulate toys, assign them characteristics, and play with the toys through a story or scene. While this appears as symbolic play, often the child is simply playing out a script or a scene most likely that he or she has watched in a movie or a TV show. The child will typically play the script or scene out over and over again with no change to the play. This should not be confused for true symbolic or pretend play. Symbolic or pretend play would typically present with the child playing out several different scenarios, using multiple toys. The scenarios will likely change often and present as a full range of expression. In true symbolic or pretend play, the child is also creating on their own, not simply playing out a scene they saw on a movie.

Children with autism spectrum disorder tend to have problems participating in social play with peers. Typically, children with ASD will become isolated in their play and withdraw from peer play groups. There is evidence to indicate that children with ASD do desire peer relationships and to participate in peer play but simply lack the social and communication skills to initiate and maintain such play. There is also evidence to indicate that children with ASD do indeed play and desire play. A child with ASD may play in nontraditional ways and may play with things that are not socially accepted as toys, but they do play.

Michael S. (an 8 year old diagnosed with ASD) is a proper example of the variability of play in children with ASD. He entered into AutPlay Therapy with a diagnosis of autism spectrum disorder, intellectual developmental disorder, and several compounding medical issues. Michael did have some verbal ability but did not speak often, and when he did, approximately 75 percent of what he said was difficult for other people to understand. The practitioner began working with Michael using the AutPlay Follow Me Approach (discussed more fully later in this chapter). Michael spent the first couple of sessions roaming around the playroom not really participating with any toys or activities in the playroom and engaging with the practitioner in limited form. The playroom that Michael had his sessions in also had a storage closet that was used to store various office supplies. Michael discovered the storage closet during Session 3.

Inside the storage closet was a vacuum cleaner. Michael quickly took notice of the vacuum cleaner and wanted to vacuum the floor and anything else he could vacuum in the playroom. The vacuum cleaner quickly became his "toy" of choice for the next several sessions. Michael would often laugh and show pure enjoyment from vacuuming. The practitioner began to incorporate skill development work using the vacuum cleaner. The practitioner created sharing games between the practitioner and Michael using the vacuum cleaner, problem solving, coping skill games, and even activities that worked on increasing eye contact and verbal expression all using Michael's interest in playing with the vacuum cleaner.

Michael's interest in playing with the office vacuum carried over to his home setting. The practitioner was able to teach Michael's parents how to use the vacuum to work on various skills. Michael's parents were able to use the vacuum cleaner at home to have play times with Michael and work on increasing targeted skill deficits. Through Michael's "vacuum play" with the practitioner and at home, Michael began to make significant strides in his treatment goals.

Each child with autism spectrum disorder or any developmental disability will have a different placement in terms of play skills. The practitioner will often not know what level or ability of play the child is going to demonstrate. It is essential that proper assessment is done to see what play ability, level, or skill a child has. It is not fair to assume that every child with ASD will not have play skills. Some children with ASD will play but in ways and with objects that may not seem like or look like traditional play. Some children with ASD do have advanced play skills, and play skills that match their neurotypical peers. It is possible to have a child who is high functioning on the autism spectrum who does engage in true pretend and imaginative play.

Children and adolescents with autism spectrum disorder and other developmental disabilities often do not track to the established developmental age charts. When deciding on directive play therapy techniques to help increase a child's skill level, it is important to remember that a child's skill level may be different from his or her chronological age. If a child or adolescent is having difficulty understanding a technique or has anxiety that is preventing him or her from completely engaging, it is important to adapt the technique so that anxiety is alleviated and engagement is increased (Delaney, 2010).

AutPlay Therapy's directive play therapy techniques are specifically designed to meet a child where he or she is in terms of his or her level of play skills. AutPlay Therapy directive play therapy techniques help increase play skills and other needed skills and abilities such as social and emotional skills. AutPlay Therapy takes into account the lack of play skills that may be present in a child with ASD and introduces play in a directive and specific manner so that children with an ASD can participate and learn from the play-based techniques. Children and adolescents are thoroughly assessed at the beginning of treatment to identify their skill deficits and assist the practitioner in creating treatment goals and choosing directive interventions to specifically address each child's skill needs.

It is important to remember that, when working with any child, using any technique, the practitioner will find that he or she participates at various levels with a child. This is determined by the practitioner when working with a child. If a child is more impaired and having trouble with the skill concept, then the practitioner will become more involved and may lead most of the technique, taking on more of an instructional and educational role. If a child is less impaired or more developed in a certain component, then the practitioner will do less directing/instructing and will let the child create and develop in the play activity on his or her own. It is important to remember that the practitioner will, at times, be very instruction/participator oriented, but the practitioner should always be looking for advancement in a child and challenging him or her to do more on his or her own.

Practitioners should take note of the AutPlay Therapy-based technique book *Play-Based Interventions for Autism and Developmental Disabilities*. This book contains over 75 directive play-based interventions and a guide for creating interventions for children with autism spectrum disorder and other developmental disorders. There are also several play-based technique books highlighted in the Appendix and the References sections at the end of this book. Although many of the referenced books are not ASD specific, some of the interventions can still be used with children and adolescents with ASD especially with some ASD-specific modifications. Some important points to remember about directive play therapy techniques with children and adolescents with ASD include:

1. Techniques should be directive or structured, meaning that the practitioner will be directing what technique to implement and will be active in the process as the technique is being implemented.
2. Techniques will have an educational component, and the practitioner will often take on an instructional role. The level of instructional role will vary from child to child depending on how much assistance is needed by the practitioner.
3. Techniques will typically avoid metaphor. Some children and adolescents with less impairment may be able to understand metaphor work, but most children and adolescents with autism spectrum disorder will not.
4. Techniques should involve a low degree or no abstract or symbolic quality. Most children and adolescents with ASD will not easily participate in or understand symbolism or abstract presentation and will accomplish more with a concrete approach.
5. Ideally, techniques should have the ability to be easily simplified or made more complex. This way, techniques can be adapted for any child or adolescent to meet each one at his or her skill level.
6. Techniques should be created that can easily be taught to parents and implemented by parents in the home setting. Parents should not be required to purchase several toys, props, or materials to implement home interventions.
7. Techniques will not always flow smoothly when being implemented. A component of directive play therapy techniques is to provide an introduction to a skill that needs to be developed. The practitioner will often stop a technique to demonstrate or talk about the correct way to say or do something.

8. Technique options are many but should always be created to work on skill development. Inspiration can be found in many places for creating techniques. Practitioners should try to create and implement techniques that will be most beneficial for the individual child or adolescent that the practitioner is working with. The Appendix contains a form guide for creating directive interventions for children with ASD.
9. Practitioners should be flexible when implementing a technique. Practitioners should be prepared to let go of the structure of the session if necessary and understand that children will likely produce an approximation of the completed technique.
10. Practitioners can use rewards and incentives to help engage a child in participating in and completing techniques. Rewards and incentives should always be discussed with the child's parents prior to using them with the child.

AutPlay Therapy is most effective for children ages 3–18 with severe to mild impairment. Children who are younger or have more impairment would begin with the Follow Me Approach discussed later in this book. Some other important guidelines to follow when conducting an AutPlay Therapy session using directive play therapy techniques with children and adolescents with autism spectrum disorder include:

1. Develop a normal routine that the child or adolescent follows as they enter the office and/or playroom to begin a session. Try to keep things the same from session to session. Children with ASD will respond more positively to things being predictable.
2. Some children and adolescents with ASD may have strong sensory issues. Practitioners should assess for these needs and adjust their office accordingly. This might include adjusting the lighting, the noise levels, being flexible in where the child wants to sit, or avoiding certain odors like a scented candle.
3. When introducing a directive play therapy technique, break down the instructions to the technique into simple understandable steps. If the child or adolescent is struggling to understand or complete an intervention, the practitioner may want to try completing one step at a time before giving the next instruction.
4. If necessary, model for the child or adolescent what you want them to do or create. Sometimes children need a visual representation of what is being asked of them. Children with ASD typically struggle with receptive language ability, so many children with ASD may struggle to understand intervention instructions if only given verbally.
5. Be prepared to participate in the play technique with the child or adolescent. Often the practitioner will be actively participating in helping the child, playing with the child, or the practitioner will be creating his or her own representation of the intervention.
6. Give the child or adolescent feedback during and after techniques to encourage and praise them for how they did and what they accomplished, especially when the child or adolescent shows skill acquisition.

7. Be an observer during the session/technique to assess if the technique seems to fit the child well and is appropriate for helping the child or adolescent reach established treatment goals. Notice if the child is struggling and try to assess how to help the child with what he or she is struggling with.

8. Ask the child questions about the technique. Ask the child or adolescent if he or she enjoyed the technique or if he or she learned anything from the technique. Try to process the technique with the child and apply the technique to the child's real life.

9. Spend some time after the session to evaluate how the session went and if the technique seems to have been successful for the child or adolescent.

10. Fun is more important than form. Children should feel safe, comfortable, and have fun during interventions. Keep in mind that children with ASD will likely experience some level of anxiety or dysregulation when addressing skill deficits.

11. A difficult-to-measure and often undervalued skill is the practitioner's playful instinct and attitude. Because many techniques involve addressing skill deficits and some techniques lack a great deal of enticement, the practitioner's playful attitude is essential for making the child's experience more engaging and enjoyable.

12. It is the relationship with the child and family that makes the techniques work best. This handbook could be filled with examples of children who challenged and struggled with other professionals who lacked a relationship focus, and yet those same children freely participated in working on all kinds of skill development with practitioners who promoted relationship development as an essential focus throughout treatment.

Once a play technique is introduced, the technique is made a part of the child's awareness from that point on. The practitioner, parents, and child may practice the same technique for several sessions in a row. A technique may be completed in one session and revisited several sessions later and completed again if it would be relevant and helpful for treatment goals or evaluation purposes. Many techniques may serve as coping and accommodation aids that the child can use throughout his or her lifetime. It is preferred that a child and parent use and reference techniques as often as appropriate. Parents can begin to accumulate a "toolbox" of ideas and interventions that they can implement with their child any time they feel it would be beneficial.

Toys, Games, and Materials

Toys, games, and expressive art materials are often used in AutPlay Therapy. (A list of suggested toys and materials for AutPlay is provided in the Appendix.) When using toys in AutPlay Therapy, there are some important issues to consider for the child or adolescent with autism spectrum disorder. First, many typical or popular toys for children or adolescents may be ignored by the child or adolescent with ASD. Second, too many toys or toys displayed in a disorganized manner may feel dysregulating to the child or adolescent with an ASD. Third, it is likely that a child or adolescent will choose to focus on one or two particular toys and want to play with them repeatedly from session to session. Fourth, more reality-based toys, such as a play phone and kitchen toys, or sensory-based toys, such as sensory balls, sand, or fidget toys, will likely be more popular or appealing for a child or adolescent with autism spectrum disorder. Finally, practitioners will want to select toys and materials that align with the directive interventions they will be implementing.

Many children and adolescents with ASD will enjoy, and may even find more appealing, games such as board games, card games, movement-based games, or prop-based games. Several AutPlay interventions do involve a game-based format. Practitioners should pay careful attention to games that involve certain skill levels or physical ability and make sure the game matches the child's ability level. Expressive materials cover a wide range of materials from art, such as painting and drawing on sand and other sensory trays or electronic apps. The main consideration in regard to expressive materials involves being sensitive to the child's sensory issues. Some children with ASD may have an aversion to the feel of sand or clay or may have a strong negative reaction to the smell of paint, while other children with ASD will not have any problems with these materials and may find them comforting and relaxing. Practitioners should pay special attention to the sensory needs of each child and adolescent when selecting interventions.

AutPlay Therapy sessions consist of directive play therapy techniques, which might involve toys, games, or expressive materials that have been selected by the practitioner as part of the directive technique. Typically, practitioners will be structuring much of the play session (an exception is the Follow Me Approach discussed later in this chapter). Purposeful toy selection is essential as it pertains to toys or materials that will be used in completing directive play therapy techniques. Practitioners should also consider that some children with ASD will want to engage in free play in the playroom setting, and these opportunities should be made available to the child. Many practitioners have successfully combined session times to include both implementing directive techniques and allowing the child time to have nondirective play time. A full list of typical toys and expressive materials can be found in the Appendix.

Play Therapy Rooms

AutPlay Therapy sessions can be facilitated in a play therapy room, practitioner's office, school counselor's office, special education classroom, or almost any environment. Since most sessions will involve preselected play therapy techniques, the practitioner can collect the materials and toys needed and have them ready in any office space. Typically, play therapy rooms include several toys and materials, so if the practitioner needs to change or adjust an intervention during a session, it will be more likely that the practitioner will have the needed materials or toys close by for an easy transition. Some children or adolescents may have a preference in regard to going into a play therapy room or to staying in the practitioner's office. If a child or adolescent has a distinct preference, then that preference should be given priority. If the child does not have a preference, then sessions might be better facilitated in a play therapy room as the play therapy room does provide a good environment and opportunity to continually evaluate and assess a child's play skills for growth and advancement. Practitioners should note that some children with ASD may find a playroom too distracting or overwhelming. If this is the case, the practitioner should facilitate sessions in his or her office or a more benign, less stimulating setting.

In AutPlay, play therapy rooms are always used during the intake and assessment phase of treatment (discussed more fully later in this book) when the practitioner conducts a child observation and a parent-and-child observation in a play therapy room. Also during the intake and assessment phase, children should be given a tour of the building, office, and playroom(s) that may be accessed. The tour helps the child become familiar with the space and gives the child the awareness that he or she can choose a playroom or some other space depending on his or her preference. After the intake and assessment phase is complete, treatment sessions can occur in any office setting as long as the needed toys and materials are present to implement interventions.

Basics of the AutPlay Therapy Process

1. AutPlay Therapy is a play therapy and behavioral therapy treatment approach for children with autism spectrum disorder, developmental disabilities, and other neurodevelopmental disorders.
2. AutPlay Therapy is most beneficial for children ages 3–18 with a severe to mild impairment level in social functioning, emotional regulation, and relationship development.
3. AutPlay Therapy involves a thorough assessment piece at the beginning of treatment to identify skill abilities and deficits.
4. Treatment focus is on skill improvement in the areas of social skills, emotional regulation, and relationship connection.
5. Directive play-based interventions are used to increase skill development.
6. Interventions are designed and implemented in regard to special learning and sensory issues that a child with ASD may be experiencing.
7. Common play therapy toys, games, and materials as well as typical play therapy rooms are utilized in treatment.
8. Parents are taught how to implement directive play-based interventions at home with their child.

AutPlay Therapy empowers the practitioner by providing a comprehensive treatment protocol that addresses the main areas that typically affect children and adolescents with autism and other developmental disabilities. Through AutPlay Therapy training, the practitioner can feel knowledgeable in the realm of autism spectrum disorder and be prepared and equipped to establish and assist in meeting treatment goals for children and adolescents with varying levels of ASD. Further, AutPlay Therapy empowers practitioners to assist parents in feeling confident and knowledgeable in helping their child gain needed skills.

AutPlay Therapy is an adaptable and compatible treatment approach for autism spectrum disorder and other developmental disabilities. AutPlay Therapy can be done in conjunction with other treatments and often is part of a collaborative approach to helping children and adolescents with ASD advance in skill development. AutPlay Therapy focuses on four component areas: emotional regulation ability, social skills development, connection (relationship development), and parent training. AutPlay Therapy consists of three phases of treatment: intake and assessment, directive play intervention, and termination. The component areas and phases are further presented and explained.

Primary Target Areas in AutPlay

Emotional Regulation Ability

When a child or adolescent is lacking emotional regulation ability, he or she has difficulty handling emotions and emotional situations. A child may become overly emotional, may not display emotions, may lack appropriate emotional expression, may not understand or be able to differentiate emotions, may not recognize emotions in others, or may not manage or control his or her own emotions. If children cannot regulate their emotions, their communication will suffer.

Children and adolescents with autism spectrum disorder and other developmental disabilities often struggle with emotional regulation. Managing and modulating both positive and negative emotions can be a challenge, and often without proper ability or training to regulate, these children and adolescents will produce negative, unwanted behaviors when they become dysregulated. Some of the signs of emotional dysregulation include mouthing or chewing on objects or fingers, holding or hording comforting objects, tip-toe walking and rocking back and forth, hand flapping, humming and making random noises, becoming aggressive or noncompliant, becoming withdrawn, attempting to remove him- or herself from a stressful situation, preoccupation with specific topics/areas of interest, and rigidness in adherence to rules or schedules.

Table 3.2 The Social, Emotional, Behavioral Process

A lack of skill development leads to ⇒	An emotional state that is poorly regulated that creates ⇒	A negative or unwanted behavior

In AutPlay Therapy, there are six categories of emotional regulation that children and adolescents with ASD may be lacking: identifying emotions, understanding and expressing emotions, emotion/situation recognition, recognizing emotions in others, sharing emotional experiences, and managing emotions. Each category can be worked on concurrently or progressively.

The six emotional regulation categories are defined below:

1. **Identifying emotions** refers to a child's ability to identify emotions, accurately label emotions, and reference several emotions as age appropriate.
2. **Understanding and expressing emotions** refers to a child's ability to understand specific emotions he or she may be experiencing, such as frustration versus anger, and being able to express the emotions that he or she is feeling in an appropriate way, such as verbally communicating his or her feelings to others.
3. **Emotion/situation recognition** refers to a child's ability to recognize that certain emotions would correspond to certain situations; for example, a woman attends a funeral, this would likely make her feel sad.
4. **Recognizing emotions in others** refers to a child's ability to recognize emotions and emotional expression in other people such as recognizing when a parent is sad or angry or when another child at school is feeling lonely.
5. **Sharing emotional experiences** refers to a child's ability to mutually participate in sharing emotion with another person, such as connecting with another in excitement while participating in a mutual activity.
6. **Managing emotions** refers to a child's overall ability to manage his or her emotions, such as identifying feelings and being able to express them in an appropriate way and understanding how to handle negative emotions to self-regulate.

Kuypers (2011) stated that self-regulation is something everyone continually works on whether they are cognizant of it or not. All people encounter trying circumstances that test their limits from time to time. If children are able to recognize when they are becoming less regulated, they will be able to do something about it to feel better and get themselves to a better place. This comes naturally for some, but for children and adolescents with autism spectrum disorder, it is a skill that needs to be taught and practiced.

In AutPlay Therapy, play-based interventions that focus on emotional regulation can be individualized to each child and adolescent to work on the regulation issues that a particular child needs to improve. Play-based interventions are natural and playful and, thus, more engaging to children. Many play-based interventions can be implemented several times, both with the practitioner and at home with parents and other family members. Play-based interventions can be implemented until the child or adolescent successfully displays the emotional regulation level or skill that is being sought. During the intake and assessment phase, a child's emotional regulation ability should be assessed using the AutPlay Emotional Regulation Ability Inventory and practitioner observations. Once a child's ability level and deficits have been assessed, directive play therapy techniques should be selected to work on the emotional regulation categories that need to be strengthened or developed.

A child's emotional regulation ability will determine which emotional regulation categories are addressed; this will vary greatly with each child with ASD. It is critical that emotional regulation is thoroughly assessed during the intake and assessment phase. Proper assessment will help identify what categories of emotional regulation a child needs to work on and will guide the practitioner in the selection of directive play therapy techniques that will be used to address the deficits. Remember that children who have more impairment will likely begin with identifying emotions, as they will be unable to master any other categories without being able to identify their emotions first. Many children with ASD begin with interventions focused on identifying or understanding and expressing emotions.

Social Skills Development

The term "social skill" actually functions as an umbrella term, covering a wide range and variety of skills from simple to more complex. Social skills can be anything from learning to make eye contact, to knowing when a situation is unsafe, to giving a speech in public.

Social skills are interpersonal, specific behaviors that permit an individual to interact successfully with others in an environment. The extent to which an individual is considered to have adequate social skills is determined by others. This is especially true for children and adolescents with autism spectrum disorder or other developmental disabilities, as they may not be able to fully understand or recognize a social skill even after they have obtained it.

Children and adolescents with ASD and other neurodevelopmental disorders have various levels of impairment in regard to social skills and social functioning. Many fail to develop age-appropriate friendships and have a great difficulty understanding the rules of social life. Laushey & Heflin (2000) suggested that impairments in social behavior are so fundamental to children with ASD that social deficits should be considered the defining feature of autism spectrum disorder.

Dawson, McPartland, & Ozonoff (2002) stated that everyone diagnosed with autism spectrum disorder has trouble with social interchange, specifically with reciprocity, the back-and-forth interaction that make up all social encounters. Further, children and adolescents with ASD tend to have a very limited concept of friendship, tend to face peer rejection, and may struggle in initiating socially encouraging body language. When children and adolescents with ASD are placed in social situations where they do not have the proper social skills to maneuver in the situation, it can create a great deal of anxiety for the child, which typically leads to unwanted behaviors. Just the thought of being put in a situation that is unfamiliar, or where there is a lack of skills to navigate successfully, can also create a great deal of anxiety and lead to unwanted behaviors.

Stillman (2007) proposed the following areas of social interaction and functioning that children and adolescents with autism spectrum disorder tend to have some level of impairment in:

1. Showing and giving affection to caregivers and other important people in the child's life.
2. What appears to be a lack of interest in making friends but actually is a lack of knowing how to engage and make friends.
3. Presenting as very shy or withdrawn.
4. A lack of understanding and recognizing irony, sarcasm, and other forms of humor.
5. A lack of being able to present and show emotions and recognize emotions in others.
6. A tendency to talk too much and about one topic.
7. Randomly talking to him- or herself in public or around others.
8. Performing stimming behavior in social situations such as chewing on his or her shirt or flapping his or her hands.
9. Seeming to be more interested in interacting with others through a computer rather than in person and wanting to spend most of his or her time playing with a computer or video game.
10. Seems to want to, and does better, talking to adults than to children his or her own age.

Dienstmann (2008) asserted that social skills must be taught. The belief that social skills magically appear in children without any development is a common misconception. Research supports social skills training as an evidence-based treatment for learning social skills. It is important to remember that social skills are skills; everyone learned them at some point. No matter where a child is at in terms of his or her current social functioning, he or she can gain additional social skills. AutPlay Therapy utilizes parents in the home setting to further develop social skills in children and adolescents with autism spectrum disorder. The opportunities to practice social skills occur each day in everyday life. Parents can provide the type of consistency and repetition needed to take advantage of daily situations to practice social skills.

AutPlay Therapy teaches children with ASD social skills and social functioning that is lacking in their current skill set. Children are first assessed to see what social skills they currently possess and what skills are in a deficit. Assessment is done by having parents and other caregivers complete the AutPlay Social Skills Inventory and by practitioner observations. Once an individual's social skill deficits have been assessed, directive play therapy techniques are chosen to work on each social skill that needs to improve. Clients are taught social skills through several directive play therapy techniques that are done in the practitioner's office or play therapy room. The directive play therapy social skills techniques are then taught to the parents to practice with their child at home.

Connection (Relationship Development)

Children with autism spectrum disorder and other neurodevelopmental disabilities do have a sense of connection and would most likely do poorly if we suddenly took away their caregivers and exchanged them for new ones. That being said, these children do have difficulty showing and expressing connection in meaningful ways and certainly have a difficult time expressing connection in socially typical and acceptable ways.

Coplan (2010) stated that children with ASD and other neurodevelopmental disorders lack reciprocity that may be evident from birth, progressing from poor eye contact as an infant or toddler, to difficulty in mastering interactive play as a preschooler, and then to an inability to see things from another person's point of view as a school-age child.

Lindaman & Booth (2010) described several difficulties that children with autism spectrum disorder have in engagement and connection:

1. Difficulties related to sensory and motor coordination making it challenging to establish rhythm and synchrony with another.
2. Less ability to imitate and anticipate another person's actions.
3. Difficulty in verbal and nonverbal communication and engaging and shifting attention create challenges in identifying feelings, thoughts, and wants.
4. Difficulties from receiving or processing information differently.
5. Difficulties making it challenging for parents to attune, understand, and respond appropriately, which can lead to more withdrawn behavior by the child.

A lack of connection and being able to feel a true sense of relationship may be one of the most troubling concerns for parents of a child with an ASD or other developmental disorder. What is happening between child and parent cannot be undervalued. Parents need to feel connection between themselves and their child, and some of that connection needs to be child initiated. Children need to learn connection in healthy and appropriate ways. Ray (2011) proposed that when children establish closeness with others they exhibit warmth toward others, seek support from adults with whom they are comfortable, and show enjoyment in their close relationships.

The connection and relationship development interventions in this book are designed to increase connection between child and caregiver; increase relationship development between child and other significant relationships; teach children and adolescents how to be more successful in engaging others and increasing relationship connections; and provide a fun, natural, play-based atmosphere for children and adolescents to master greater relationship and connection skills.

The connection and relationship development interventions in this book range from simple to more complex by design. Practitioners should pay special attention to the functioning level and age of the child they are working with and choose interventions that match the child's level. Children who have a lower functioning level will likely struggle with the most basic connection-based intervention and may start participating at a minimal level. It is important and appropriate to work with the child's level and progress forward with the child. Forcing a child or adolescent to participate in a connection-based intervention that he or she is uncomfortable with or that is beyond his or her functioning level, will likely result in the child having a behavior "meltdown" and may result in the child being even more resistant to participating in future connection-based interventions.

Children and adolescents with autism spectrum disorder and other neuro-developmental disorders seem to universally have a desire for greater connection with others and a longing to have deeper relationship experiences at least to a level that they feel comfortable with. Consequently, almost universally, children dealing with these issues are not experiencing the level of connection and relationship that they desire and seem to lack the skill level or ability to attain the level of connection they would like to have.

Through consistent and purposeful introduction and practice of play-based interventions designed to increase a child's skill level and ability in making and keeping meaningful connections and relationships, practitioners and parents can help children and adolescents reach the level of connection and relationship development that they desire. It is likely that each child and adolescent will present with a different goal level in terms of how much connection skill they develop and what level of relationship each child and adolescent is seeking and comfortable with. It is not necessary for every person, atypical or neurotypical, to possess the same desire and skill level in relationship development. There is some subjectivity that should be implemented in determining what level of connection ability each child and adolescent may need for general functioning purposes and what level they may want to achieve in terms of greater connection and relationship development with others.

The AutPlay Therapy connection component focuses on creating directive play therapy techniques that parent and child can do together that help foster relationship development and connection. These techniques are designed to be fun and connecting for both parent and child and to be directive in helping children learn relationship connection and development skills.

It is important to note that, in regard to the connection component area, there is connection work happening when parents are implementing the directive play therapy techniques related to emotional regulation and social skills. Some connection work is organically being produced when parents are working on these two component areas even when the connection component area is not specifically being addressed. Thus, connection is actually being addressed and developed throughout the entire AutPlay Therapy process.

Secondary Target Areas in AutPlay

AutPlay Therapy treatment protocol not only targets three primary areas but also three secondary target areas, which include anxiety reduction, sensory processing improvement, and behavioral change. Parker & O'Brien (2011) noted that some studies have indicated that children and adolescents with ASD have high levels of depression and anxiety. Children and adolescents with ASD and other developmental disorders often experience a great deal of anxiety, which leads to dysregulation and unwanted behaviors. Much of the anxiety is produced by a lack of skill development. Often, these children and adolescents lack sufficient skills in handling social situations or sufficient skills in managing their own emotional states. When appropriate and specific play-based interventions can be implemented, children and adolescents can learn the skills needed to function in a variety of settings and emotional states and have the ability to regulate themselves through scenarios that might otherwise be dysregulating.

Sensory processing consists of the stimulation that a child is continuously receiving through his or her senses, which include visual, auditory, tactile, gustatory, olfactory, vestibular, and proprioceptive stimulation (Obrey & Barboa, 2014). Children and adolescents with ASD often struggle with sensory processing issues. Many of the environments that children and adolescents with ASD find themselves in are often extremely stimulating to one or more of the seven senses. The extreme sensitivities and struggles with processing sensory stimuli can easily lead to behavioral meltdowns. Cross (2010) offered that children who are provided play experiences that are intentionally planned with the seven senses of sensory integration in mind are capable of, not only overcoming play and learning difficulties, but also pushing their abilities and exceeding expectations.

Vaughan (2014) stated that all behavior is a message. It paints a picture of what the child is thinking and feeling and reflects how he or she is processing information from the world. Children and adolescents with ASD often do produce unwanted behaviors usually in regard to being in a dysregulated state. For children with ASD, a dysregulated state can be influenced by a myriad of skill deficits and environmental conditions. Miller & Smith (2014) proposed that a dysregulated state can happen due to a variety of conditions including difficulty making transitions and handling change, sensory processing challenges, an inability to cope with social demands and expectations, and an inability to regulate emotional states. Most unwanted behavior from a child with ASD, especially dysregulated meltdowns, is understood to be involuntary and largely due to social and communication skill deficits.

AutPlay Therapy addresses the secondary target areas of anxiety reduction, sensory processing, and behavioral change through established AutPlay treatment protocol. Directive interventions that have a specific emotional regulation component will help children regulate their emotional states and decrease anxiety. Social skill interventions will help children not only gain skills for various social situations, but possessing these skills will reduce anxiety and help children avoid dysregulated states. Many AutPlay connection and emotional regulation interventions incorporate a sensory processing component. When there is skill improvement in the three primary target areas, this will lead to anxiety reduction and sensory processing ability, which all leads to improving unwanted behavior.

Treatment Phases in AutPlay

Intake and Assessment Phase

The intake and assessment phase of AutPlay Therapy typically lasts four sessions. (An intake and assessment guide is provided for practitioners in the Appendix.) The first session is a general intake session with the parents. Typically, children are not involved in this session. The practitioner meets with the parents to complete all necessary paperwork and to acquire information on presenting issues and on the child/family background. The practitioner explains the therapy process and explains how AutPlay Therapy works. The practitioner provides the parents with the AutPlay Emotional Regulation Inventory, the AutPlay Social Skills Inventory, the AutPlay Connection Inventory, and the AutPlay Assessment of Play Inventory to complete. The practitioner may give parents additional inventories to complete if it is deemed necessary. A helpful additional inventory might include the Autism Treatment Evaluation Checklist (ATEC), which is free and can be printed off and scored online at www.autism.com.

Session 2 involves the practitioner working one-on-one with the child. The practitioner will meet with the child to begin to establish a relationship and help the child feel familiar and comfortable with therapy. The practitioner will also informally observe/assess the child. Typically, this is done in a play therapy room. The play therapy room provides a wonderful opportunity to assess developmental levels and play development in children with autism spectrum disorder and other developmental disabilities. The practitioner will use and complete the AutPlay Child Observation Form to help conceptualize the child's skill and functioning levels. The practitioner and child will typically participate in the observation time for the entire session, approximately 45 minutes. The practitioner should focus on relationship- and rapport-building as well as completing the questions on the AutPlay Child Observation Form.

Session 3 involves both parent and child. The practitioner will observe the child and parent together in a play therapy room. If possible, the practitioner will observe via a monitor or two-way mirror. If this type of process is not available, then the practitioner should stay in one corner of the play therapy room and try to observe only. The child/parent observation should last approximately 25 minutes. The remaining time should be used for the practitioner to meet with the parent and review observations and answer questions. If the child cannot stay by him- or herself in the waiting area, then the practitioner should discuss with the parent before the third session that childcare will need to be arranged while the parent and practitioner meet. During the child/parent observation, the practitioner should use and complete the AutPlay Child/Parent Observation Form to help conceptualize the child's skill and functioning levels.

The observation can include both parents with the child or one parent with the child. Parents may feel anxious about being observed. Practitioners should help parents feel comfortable and explain that they are free to do whatever they would normally do at home and that there are no limits other than keeping the child safe. It should be explained to the parents that the observation will last about 25 minutes and that the remaining time will be spent going through the inventories and discussing the observations.

Parents should have completed and returned all inventories given to them from the practitioner by Session 3. Between Session 3 and Session 4, the practitioner should review the parent-completed inventories and observation forms. The practitioner should complete the AutPlay Treatment Plan Profile, selecting what target areas and specific skills to address. The practitioner will then select directive play therapy techniques to use to work on the target areas and specific skills chosen.

Session 4 begins with the practitioner meeting with the child for the first half of the session to continue to build relationship and help the child gain familiarity and feel comfortable. The second half of the session involves the practitioner meeting with the parents to review the treatment plan and to establish the directive play intervention phase of the therapy. The practitioner should explain the treatment process, what component area is going to be addressed first, what specific skills will be addressed, and how treatment will progress. This is a time for discussion with the parents. The practitioner will want to make sure the parents are in agreement with the treatment plan.

During Session 4, the practitioner will also establish with the parents how the alternating sessions between parents and child will occur. Session times with the practitioner will alternate between child and parents. This can happen in several ways. The most common way is meeting with the parents one week and then meeting with the child the next week. If it is possible to meet twice in one week, then one time can be with the child and the other with the parents. Another possible combination is meeting each week with both parent and child by dividing the session time. This should be explained, and the meeting cycle established.

Directive Play Intervention Phase

The intake and assessment phase is basically a time to establish what will happen during the directive play intervention phase. Once this has been established, the directive play intervention phase begins. This tends to begin around Session 5 and starts with a parent session. During the parent session, the practitioner will explain the play therapy technique that will be taught and used with the child in the next session. The practitioner explains and practices the technique with the parents and discusses how they will implement it at home. The practitioner gives the parents the instructions for what they will be expected to do with their child after the next child session. Parents will not actually begin implementing the technique at home until the practitioner has had a session with the child and has explained and practiced the technique with the child in session.

Session 6 is a session with the child. The child is taught a directive play therapy technique, and the technique is practiced in session. The practitioner explains to the child that his or her parents will be working with him or her for the next two weeks, playing the technique at home. At the end of the session, the practitioner reminds the parents that they will now be implementing the technique at home and that the child has been made aware of this by the practitioner. The alternating between parent and child sessions and sessions teaching play therapy techniques is the main cycle of the directive play intervention phase. This continues until treatment goals are met. As much as possible, parents should be taught how to do the directive play therapy techniques at home that the practitioner is doing with the child in session. There will be some directive play therapy techniques that the practitioner does with the child in session that may not, by nature of the design of the activity, transfer to the home setting. This is allowed but should be in the minority. The majority of the play therapy techniques should be taught to the parents and transferred to the home environment.

The length of the directive play intervention phase varies. How much time is spent during the directive play intervention phase will depend on the function and skill level the child begins at and the level of participation the parents provide. The higher the skill level to begin with and the more parent participation, the quicker the directive play intervention phase will progress. It is important to let parents know that there is not a set number of sessions for the directive play intervention phase. Children participating in single case study designs have shown a marked improvement in the three AutPlay component areas of emotional regulation ability, social skills development, and connection after 6 months. This does not indicate an end to the directive play intervention phase but rather a guide to showing improvement and progress toward treatment goals.

Practitioners should implement an evaluation process and periodically re-evaluate to make sure treatment goals are being met and to assess the need for additional treatment goals. One approach would be to have parents complete updated inventories from the first session and compare parent ratings from the initial inventories and the current ones. As improvement is made and treatment goals are being met, it may be appropriate to lessen the parent sessions to once per month and have more session times with the child. If parents have learned most of the techniques and are actively and accurately implementing the techniques at home, then session times with the parents can be limited to once per month until treatment is terminated, but meeting times with parents should continue on some level until treatment is terminated. Remember that the combination of parent-training sessions and child sessions can be implemented in a variety of ways. Practitioners may find it more feasible to meet with the child and parents together each session or to divide the session in half meeting the first half with the child and second half with the parents.

Termination Phase

Using the AutPlay Treatment Plan Profile as a guide, the practitioner and the parents will assess when treatment goals have been meet. At this point, the termination phase begins. The termination phase usually consists of three sessions. The first session is a session with the parents to review the treatment plan and assess whether treatment goals have adequately been accomplished and there are no other treatment goals to work on. It is important to note that the initial treatment plan will likely be updated by the practitioner and parents throughout the directive play intervention phase with new goals being added. The termination phase begins when the practitioner and parents meet to review the treatment goals and establish that goals have been met and there are no new goals to accomplish. The practitioner will review with the parents what they have learned and how to maintain the progress they have made. The practitioner will emphasize with the parents the importance of continuing to facilitate the learning of skills with the techniques they have gained.

Session 2 of the termination phase is a session with the child. The practitioner will explain to the child that sessions will be ending and review with the child what he or she has learned. The practitioner will encourage the child to continue using techniques that he or she has gained. The practitioner will explain to the child that the next session will be the last session and will include the parents in a "graduation party" session.

Session 3 of the termination phase is the final session and includes parents, the child, and any other family members that the child would like to invite. This session is a graduation party for the child. The emphasis should be positive, fun, and focused on how much the child has accomplished and has now graduated from therapy. Typically, the party is held in the practitioner's office, a play therapy room, or any space that is decorated with party decorations and balloons. A graduation cake is provided, and other components may be included such as a small graduation gift, additional food, etc. The practitioner and parents should plan the party together. Proper goodbyes are given at the graduation party, and the parents and child are reminded that they may contact the practitioner at any time if they have questions or need to resume therapy.

Parent Training

AutPlay Therapy incorporates a parent-training component that teaches parents how to conduct directive play therapy techniques at home. Parents learn the procedures and techniques and are shown how to implement techniques at home to increase skill and ability levels in their child. Around Session 3 or 4, the practitioner will begin to alternate sessions between the parent and the child. This may be done by meeting one week with the parents and the next week meeting with the child, or this may be done by having two sessions in one week—one with parents and one with the child. In some cases, parent and child might participate together in the same session and learn the intervention at the same time. Having the parent and child together in a session while teaching a skill intervention should be given careful consideration. There may be topics to discuss or explanations that need to be covered with the parent that would not be appropriate for the child to be present. The arrangement will depend on several factors, such as scheduling and billing, but there should be some type of parent participation to adequately train parents.

During the parent sessions, the practitioner will review how things are going at home and ask the parents for an update on any homework techniques or assignments the parents have been implementing. The practitioner will also discuss with the parents any new techniques to begin at home and any new homework assignments. During a parent session, it is common for the practitioner to engage with the parents concerning their own process in parenting their child. Often, practitioners will listen to and counsel parents regarding their own struggles or concerns in parenting a child with a developmental disability. While this may be a component, it should not consume the entire parent session. It is important that the parent sessions cover the techniques and homework assignments that the parents need to be doing at home with their child. If it seems like the parents would benefit from, or need their own couples or individual counseling, then a referral should be made for such intervention.

In AutPlay Therapy, the ultimate goal in regard to parent involvement is to have parents become co-change agents with the practitioner. Parents should be encouraged, supported, and feel empowered to work with their child in ways that will be productive to established treatment goals. The practitioner is training the parents to do directive play therapy techniques at home with their child. These techniques are typically chosen by the practitioner (although parents can participate in choosing techniques) as techniques to use to help develop skill deficits in the three component areas that have been assessed: emotional regulation ability, social skills development, and connection. The practitioner will continue to meet with parents and train parents on implementing the techniques at home until treatment goals have been met. It may be appropriate, after a certain length of time, to reduce parent meetings to once per month, but parent meetings should continue at some level until therapy has been terminated.

Home interventions mimic what the practitioner is doing with the child in sessions. If the practitioner has a session with the child and incorporates the Me and My Feelings intervention, then the parents are taught how to do this intervention at home and given an expectation of completing the intervention at home between counseling sessions. When an intervention is taught to parents and sent home, it is most helpful to give parents and child specific instruction in regard to completing the intervention home. An example of a specific instruction might be "Complete the Me and My Feelings intervention three times before our next session, or complete the intervention once a day before our next session." Providing this time expectation will give parents a better guideline to follow and be more productive in ensuring that parents will complete the interventions at home.

AutPlay Therapy offers a great deal of flexibility in working with parents and the parent-training component. If there are two parents involved, then both parents can be trained at the same time, or parent training can involve only one parent. The term "parent" is used openly. The parent figure is typically worked with during parent trainings. This is the primary caregiver for the child. This may be a foster parent, adoptive parent, grandparent, a residential facility case manager, or whoever is primarily involved with and raising the child. It is also important to try and involve other family members or others who are active in the child's life. For example, if there is an older sibling in the family, then at some point that sibling might be brought into the parent-training time and taught how to implement interventions at home with the child. This could also be done with a grandparent, aunt, uncle, or any family member who is actively involved with the child.

Before involving another family member, it will be necessary to discuss with the parents and assess for appropriateness. The other family member will need to be someone who could be taught the interventions and would be capable and appropriate to work with the child. If it appears that the other family member in question would not work well with the child, then that family member should not be incorporated into the training process. When appropriate and possible, practitioners should try to incorporate other family members as this will provide additional support for the parents, relieve some of the implementation responsibility from parents, and help the child generalize working on skill development with a variety of people.

For practitioners working in a school setting or other setting where access to parents may not be an option, trying to incorporate other professionals who work with the child is an appropriate alternative. Some examples might be a paraprofessional, another teacher, or an intern. The goal would be to include one or more people so the child could practice the intervention multiple times between meeting times with the primary practitioner. Ideally, there would be parent involvement, but if parental involvement is not possible, then incorporating other professionals to ensure the repetitive practice of skill interventions would be appropriate.

It is appropriate to incorporate into the parent-training sessions traditional parenting skills training that might be beneficial. Some examples might include Love and Logic, 123 Magic, Nurtured Heart, or any parenting approach that would have elements helpful for parenting a child with autism spectrum disorder or any other developmental disability. It is important to be aware that many popular parenting programs are designed for neurotypical children and may have components that are not helpful or beneficial for a child with ASD or other developmental disabilities. The practitioner should fully understand both the child with ASD and the parenting approach they are teaching to apply elements that would be helpful for parenting a child with ASD or other developmental disability.

It is likely that the parent-training sessions will cover some level of behavior modification approaches. This might include teaching parents how to set up a weekly visual schedule for their child, developing routine and consistency, establishing appropriate consequences, and how to implement consequences and reward systems. The AutPlay Situation Behavior Assessment can be completed by the practitioner, parents, or others observing the child's behavior. This inventory can be helpful in identifying what might be causing particular behaviors and what might be implemented to help decrease the negative behaviors.

Practitioners can also use the AutPlay Unwanted Behaviors Inventory to help identify what types of behavior issues are happening at home and at school. This will help practitioners identify what types of behavior change strategies or parenting approaches to share with parents to help decrease unwanted behaviors. Practitioners unaware of basic behavioral therapy strategies, especially those involving children, should spend time reading, participating in additional trainings, or participating in professional development opportunities to become more familiar with behavioral therapy approaches.

Practitioner's Checklist for Parent-Training Sessions

1. Review with parents how the home play intervention has been going. How often did they implement the intervention? Did things go smoothly? Were there any problems? What were observed outcomes? Did the child participate and seem to gain from the intervention?
2. Update on the child's behavior at home and at school.
3. Cover any issues or questions that the parents may have about AutPlay, home behaviors, parenting strategies, or school issues.
4. Work on and teach any specific parenting strategies or behavior modification techniques if applicable.
5. Teach parents any new interventions to do with the child before the next session. Remember that parents are learning as the child learns, so when the practitioner completes a new intervention with the child in session, then parents should be taught to implement that same intervention at home.

Considerations with Home Interventions

The parent and child implementation of play interventions at home is a critical piece of the AutPlay Therapy process. Some special considerations or issues may occur when interventions are implemented at home. Being at home can provide a familiarity and comfort that might not be the same in a clinical office setting. While this can be positive, it can also present a challenge to implementing home interventions. Families may not take the interventions as seriously or present the interventions in enough of a formal process so that the intervention becomes less than a watered-down approach compared to the interventions being implemented by the practitioner with the child in a counseling session. This would be something to assess and take note of during parent sessions when gaining feedback. If this is happening, parents should be encouraged to try and present the interventions fully and with a purposeful intention, possibly even adding a formal piece such as establishing with the practitioner when, how, and where interventions are going to be done at home.

Another possible home issue would be distractions and disruptions. The home environment will likely be less controlled than the practitioner's office.

Families may have other children or even other relatives in the home. There may be a challenge to finding space and time where the parent can exclusively focus on and implement an intervention with the child. This is something the practitioner would address with the parent and try to establish with the parent for the best possible option with the least amount of distractions or disruptions. Practitioners may discover that parents are implementing the interventions in a modified version. This could be due to time restraint issues, not fully understanding the intervention when it was explained, not remembering the instructions, or a variety of other reasons. Practitioners will want to address this issue and make sure parents are accurately implementing interventions at home. If interventions are not being implemented at home, practitioners will want to discover why this is happening and focus on helping parents become successful with home implementation. When introducing interventions to parents, practitioners should make sure to present the intervention verbally, in written form (provide a handout detailing the intervention or have the parents write down the instructions), and practice the intervention with parents. This will help ensure proper implementation in the home setting.

Occasionally, parents may find that they have a more challenging time getting their child to participate with them in the play intervention at home than is experienced by the practitioner working with the child in the practitioner's office. This would be important feedback to acquire during parent sessions and discussed with parents in terms of implementing strategies to help with home compliance. The practitioner may want to address this with the child and more formally explain to the child that he or she will be participating with his or her parent at home and be expected to come back to the next session and bring in any materials created and discuss what he or she did with his or her parents at home. Parents may also have difficulty with providing materials at home that are needed to complete various play interventions. If parents are struggling to provide the needed materials, the practitioner should try to provide interventions that require little or no materials or assist parents with ideas for acquiring the needed materials.

A common issue echoed by AutPlay Practitioners is what to do when parents do not participate. For a variety of reasons, a practitioner may encounter a parent who does not participate in implementing interventions at home. Parental lack of participation can manifest from a variety of reasons: Parents may be too busy, parents may have good intensions but live a very hectic life and have a challenge scheduling in an intervention, parents may feel inadequate to implement interventions at home, parents may believe the interventions will not help, or a variety of other reasons.

If possible, practitioners should try to discover what is creating the lack of parental participation and try to resolve the issue. If all else fails, and there is a lack of parental participation, practitioners should continue to work with the child and try to make as much gain as possible. Practitioners may try to incorporate other professionals to work with the child such as an intern or try to have multiple sessions each week with the child. Parent participation is a critical piece to fully implementing AutPlay Therapy, but for a variety of reasons, there may be situations where there is no parental participation. Children still deserve treatment even if this means referring them to another type of treatment provider that might better meet their needs.

Addressing Parent Lack of Participation

1. Provide empathy, encouragement, and support. Treat parents with respect and as co-change agents with the practitioner.
2. Address the lack of participation and assess what might be creating the lack of participation. Listen to parents' issues and concerns, brainstorm, and work with parents to rectify the issues that are creating a lack of participation.
3. Educate parents about autism issues and the best treatment approaches that include parental involvement.
4. Educate about the importance of empowering parents and providing parents with lifelong tools to work with and help their child.
5. Discuss with parents that the AutPlay treatment process will be much slower in reaching treatment goals if there is a lack of parent participation.
6. Discuss with parents the possibility of other family members participating in treatment and working with the child at home.

Parents of children with autism spectrum disorder or other developmental disabilities often find themselves in a life that requires a high degree of focus and attention with little or no respite or opportunity for much needed self-care. Some research has suggested that the stress and anxiety levels of parents with a child with ASD can equal those levels of someone with posttraumatic stress disorder (PTSD). A common discussion during parent trainings involves discussing with parents the concept of self-care. Some parents may understand the benefits and necessity of self-care and are already producing regular self-care into their lifestyle. Other parents (unfortunately many) may not understand what self-care looks like and how to implement self-care into their life. The AutPlay Parent Self-Care Inventory can be useful in identifying self-care resources and options for parents. Practitioners should address parent self-care at some point with parents and identify if parents currently have self-care resources and options in place and if not, process with parents to establish self-care resources and strategies.

Follow Me Approach (For Children with Greater Functional and Skill Impairments)

Directive play therapy techniques are central to the AutPlay Therapy process. With most directive play therapy techniques, the technique can be adjusted to be more simple or more complex depending on the child's age and functioning level. The adjustment from simple to complex does not affect the quality of the technique in being effective for helping children and adolescents improve skill levels. It is important to begin work at the child's functioning and skill level and advance forward.

Children and adolescents with ASD plot on a functioning and skill spectrum from severe impairment to mild impairment. Children and adolescents who have a severe impairment, or who are lower functioning in skill level, may have a difficult time attuning to and participating in directive techniques even when the techniques are simplified. For these children, the Follow Me Approach would be appropriate.

The Follow Me Approach is used with children who have a functioning level that creates issues with focusing on and being able to participate in directive play therapy techniques. During the intake and assessment phase, through observation and assessment, it will become clear to the practitioner if a child is at a level that requires the Follow Me Approach. If this is the case, then the Follow Me Approach will be the main technique that will be implemented from session to session until more directive interventions can be implemented. Parents will be taught how to conduct a Follow Me Approach play time at home, and during implementation of the Follow Me Approach, the practitioner will continually be progressing toward implementing more directive techniques.

What Is the Follow Me Approach?

The Follow Me Approach focuses on relationship development, skill development, and moving the child from an inability to focus and complete directive instruction to participating fully in practitioner- and parent-led directive play techniques.

The practitioner and child participate in a typical play therapy room. The child is given no directive instructions from the practitioner. The practitioner follows the child's lead, moving with the child around the room and trying to engage with the child in whatever activity he or she is doing. The practitioner lets the child lead but always gets involved with what the child is doing. The practitioner transitions as the child transitions. The practitioner is continuously looking for opportunities to connect with the child through eye contact, verbalizations, or any other goals that are being worked on. As the child transitions from one toy or activity to another, the practitioner transitions with the child.

Throughout the session, the practitioner is using reflecting and tracking statements and being mindful of the child's comfort level. In the Follow Me Approach, it is important to not only share physical space with the child, but also share attention, emotion, and understanding with the child. Initially, a child with autism spectrum disorder may find the Follow Me Approach uncomfortable and the experience of someone trying to connect or engage with him or her intrusive. If a child starts to become agitated or dysregulated by the practitioner's attempts to get involved with what he or she is doing, then the practitioner should discontinue attempts to get involved and simply stay present with the child providing reflecting and tracking statements. The practitioner may begin to engage the child once the child seems to feel comfortable. A typical session time with a child using the Follow Me Approach would last approximately 25 minutes. The remainder of the session should be spent processing with the parent.

When parents are taught the Follow Me Approach, it will be helpful for them to watch the practitioner conducting the Follow Me Approach with their child in sessions. Parents should be observing the Follow Me Approach sessions the practitioner is having with the child. When parents implement the approach at home, they are instructed to try and have a Follow Me play time every day for approximately 25 minutes. This is an ideal scenario, parents and practitioners should be flexible with the length of time and the number of times that the approach can be implemented at home. When deciding how many play times to have and the length of the play times, consideration should be given to the child's ability to participate. During practitioner process times with the parents, the practitioner will review with the parents how the Follow Me play times are going at home and address any questions or concerns parents may have.

When the child has sessions with the practitioner, the practitioner will conduct the Follow Me sessions and continuously be looking for opportunities to introduce more directive play therapy techniques. This is a testing out time to see if the child is yet capable of engaging in some directive play therapy techniques. If the child responds well, then the practitioner will continue to introduce more directive techniques. If the child does not respond well, the practitioner will continue with the Follow Me Approach and keep looking for opportunities to introduce more directive play therapy techniques.

Practitioners should be continually looking for improvement in the child's functioning level to the point of the child being able to participate in directive play therapy techniques. A child should not stay in the Follow Me Approach indefinitely. The Follow Me Approach is a beginning approach to lead to the child participating in more directive play therapy techniques. It is important to note that typically if a child is at a functioning level where the Follow Me Approach is going to be implemented, it is likely that the child will need other concurrent treatments in addition to AutPlay Therapy. Such treatments might include occupational therapy, speech therapy, and applied behavioral analysis interventions.

Implementing the Follow Me Approach

This technique is predominantly used when a child's developmental and functional level is such that he or she will not participate in any directive techniques. The practitioner begins by introducing the child to the playroom. The practitioner explains to the child that, "This is a playroom, and you can do whatever you like in here, and I will be in here with you." No rules or limits are established at this time.

The child is allowed to roam around the playroom and play with or attend to anything he or she likes. The child is also allowed to switch from toy to toy as he or she likes. The child leads the time, and the practitioner follows the child and tries to become involved and engage the child in whatever the child is doing. As the child is playing, the practitioner should periodically be:

1. Making tracking and reflective statements.
2. Asking questions.
3. Trying to engage with the child in his or her play or activity.
4. Looking for advancement in skill development, especially attunement skills such as making eye contact, reciprocal play, acknowledging the practitioner, and asking and answering questions.
5. Looking for opportunities to engage the child in a therapist-led directive game or activity.
6. Developing relationship with the child through tracking and reflective statements, being present with the child, and setting limits.

Tracking and reflection statements should be done intermittently to communicate presence with the child and enable better relationship development. Tracking statements are simple statements about what the child is doing. Some example tracking statements include "You are finished with the sand tray, and now you are playing with the doll," or "You are hammering that really hard." Reflection statements are made by the practitioner to identify a feeling that the practitioner perceives is coming from the child. Some example reflecting statements include "Blowing the bubbles makes you feel happy" or "You don't like it when I move the cars."

Practitioners should regularly ask the child questions. The questions can be about anything. Some example questions might be "Do you have any brothers at home?" "Do you like to play with blocks?" or "What color is that?" It is likely that many questions will not garner a response from the child. Many children may not even acknowledge they have been asked a question. The practitioner is asking questions to identify when a child begins to answer questions and how well and often a child answers questions. When a child begins to answer questions regularly and fully, it is an indication the child is attuning more to the practitioner and is moving toward being able to do more directive techniques.

Throughout a Follow Me session, the practitioner is trying to engage with the child in whatever the child is doing. Remember that the child leads and chooses whatever the child wants to play with, but the practitioner follows the child and tries to get involved with what the child is doing. The practitioner should make several attempts throughout the session. If the child responds and engages with the practitioner, the practitioner should continue with whatever is being done until the child is no longer interested. If the child begins to show irritation or dysregulation with the attempts the practitioner is making to engage, then the practitioner should stop trying to engage and move away from the child and simply make some tracking and reflecting statements for about 5 minutes and then return to trying to engage with the child.

The practitioner should be sensitive to the child's comfort level. Some sessions may be mostly tracking and reflecting statements if the child is displaying discomfort with the practitioner's attempts to engage. The practitioner should not try to engage or get involved with what the child is doing to the point where the child becomes fully dysregulated and has a meltdown. Some examples of engaging with the child include:

1. The child starts playing with the play dishes. The practitioner sits beside the child, takes a bowl, puts it on the practitioner's head, and says to the child, "Look at my silly bowl hat." The practitioner is trying to engage the child by having the child look at the practitioner and notice the bowl on the practitioner's head. The practitioner might take a bowl or plate and put it on the child's head and say, "Look at the plate on your head." The practitioner might ask the child to put a bowl or plate on the practitioner's head and see if they can begin to engage in this activity back and forth.

2. The child starts playing with the sand tray pouring sand into a bucket. The practitioner moves beside the child and starts pouring sand into the same bucket. The practitioner then might try to pour sand on the child's arm or hand and might try to bury the child's hand in the sand. Another attempt would be to try and get the child to pour sand into the practitioner's hand.

3. The child starts to play with rolling some cars around on the floor. The practitioner sits down beside the child and starts rolling some cars with the child. The child grabs the cars from the practitioner and pushes the practitioner away. This is a sign the child may not feel comfortable with what the practitioner is doing or the child may be becoming dysregulated. The practitioner should move away from the child and observe the child making some periodic tracking and reflecting statements and try to engage with the child again in approximately 5 minutes.

The practitioner will want to always be looking for some advancement or display of skill acquisition. Prior to beginning the Follow Me Approach, the practitioner, along with the parents, should identify and establish some basic attuning and acknowledgment skills to work toward with the Follow Me Approach. Some common examples might include making eye contact, responding to questions, making verbalizations, initiating with the practitioner, engaging with the practitioner, displaying joint attention, asking the practitioner a question, etc. The practitioner should take note of instances where the pre-identified skills occur and seem to happen more frequently or the child has mastered the skill with the practitioner. Accomplishment of these skills is another indication that the child is moving toward being able to participate in more directive techniques.

The ultimate goal in the follow Me Approach is to help the child acquire to a level of functioning where he or she can participate with the practitioner in more directive techniques that focus on skill improvement. The practitioner should periodically initiate and see if the child will participate in a more directive game or activity with the practitioner. As the child begins to do this with the practitioner, the practitioner can begin to advance the games or activities and increase the child's level of participation.

Practitioner's Guide for Implementing the Follow Me Approach

The practitioner should:

Follow the child: The child leads and the practitioner follows the child figuratively and literally. The practitioner lets the child move around the playroom and lets the child play with anything that he or she wants. The practitioner moves with the child, sits by the child, and transitions as the child transitions.

Make tracking statements: The practitioner makes these statements periodically tracking what the child is doing, for example, "You are playing in the sand tray," "You just shot the Nerf gun," or "You are looking around at all the toys in here."

Make reflecting statements: The practitioner makes these statements when the practitioner notices a child displaying a feeling, for example, "That makes you mad" or "You feel sad that there is no more paint."

Ask questions: The practitioner should periodically ask the child questions. The practitioner should try to ask questions that are relevant. For example, if the child picks up a basketball, the practitioner might ask, "Do you have a basketball at home?"

Attempt to engage the child: The practitioner should frequently try to engage the child or play with the child in whatever he or she is doing. For example, if the child is playing in the sand tray, the practitioner might try scooping up some sand and pouring it on the child's hand or scooping up some sand and putting it in the bucket the child is trying to fill. Another example might be, if the child is playing with some balls, the practitioner might pick up a ball and try to roll it or toss it to the child.

Introduce simple directive games: The practitioner should periodically introduce a simple directive game or activity to see if the child will participate with the practitioner. This is somewhat of a "testing out" process to evaluate if the child is making progress toward participating in more directive interventions.

Monitor for dysregulation: The practitioner should be sensitive to the child's comfort level especially in regard to engaging with the child. If the practitioner notices that the child is becoming uncomfortable or dysregulated by the practitioner's attempts to engage, the practitioner should discontinue making attempts to engage and move away from the child for a period of time and then try again.

Be mindful of goals: The practitioner is working on relationship development and increasing the child's comfort level being present with the practitioner. The practitioner is looking for ways to connect and signs of the child responding to or connecting with the practitioner. This might be through verbalizations or playing together or making eye contact. The practitioner should never try to force engaging or a connection. If the child is showing they are not interested, then the practitioner should do some tracking statements for a while and try engaging again later. The practitioner is ultimately looking for signs that the child is ready to participate in more directive techniques with the practitioner.

Follow Me to Connecting Sets to Directive Techniques

As the Follow Me Approach begins to lead to the child and practitioner engaging freely in more directive activities, the practitioner should move the process into what are called *connecting sets*. Connecting sets are a natural next step or middle step between the Follow Me Approach and directive techniques. Connecting sets are focused on skill improvement and consist of a set of several short, fun, engaging games between the practitioner and the child. Each game requires a simple level of instruction and participation with the practitioner.

Connecting sets should consist of several games/activities that last approximately 15–20 minutes. The activities should be short and simple and have a connection component. Activities will likely begin slowly with little or no response from the child. Practitioners should continue with the activities and look for the child to gradually increase his or her participation with the practitioner. The practitioner should have several connecting games to choose from and introduce to the child, as the child will likely respond more positively to some versus others. The practitioner and child may play one activity for 30 seconds and another for 5 minutes. This will vary and depend on the child's interest. In the beginning of introducing connecting set games, it is likely the connecting set time will not reach 15–20 minutes. The child may start by only participating with the practitioner for 5 minutes. The practitioner can work toward building up to a 15–20 minute connecting set time.

A connecting set example might be that the practitioner identifies that the child is ready to start participating in more directive engagement with the practitioner. The practitioner introduces connecting sets. The practitioner introduces a balloon toss to the child, hitting a balloon back and forth. The first time balloon toss is introduced, the child hits the balloon back once and then leaves the activity and plays by himself. The next session the practitioner tries the balloon toss game again. This time the child hits the balloon back 3 times; by the fourth session, the child is hitting the balloon back 10 times before becoming disinterested. During the fourth session, after the balloon toss game, the practitioner immediately introduces a second connecting set game: bubble blowing and popping. The child participates with the practitioner blowing the bubbles and the child popping the bubbles for approximately

5 minutes. By the seventh session of introducing connecting sets, the child is participating in approximately 15 minutes' worth of connecting set games with the practitioner.

Connecting set games do not have to be designated therapeutic games. The practitioner has a wide range of options available when introducing a connecting game. The primary goal is to have the child participating with the practitioner or parent in a simple game that requires a level of following instruction, attunement, and acknowledgment. Some examples might include hitting a balloon back and forth; lotion games; thumb wrestling; playing hand games such as patty cake; feeding games; throwing, rolling, or kicking a ball back and forth; playing hide and seek; playing chase and catch; mirroring games; bubble-blowing games; Play Doh games; movement games such as duck, duck, goose; and hand games.

The Follow Me Approach is a beginning approach with the goal of moving into more directive interventions. Throughout the Follow Me Approach, the practitioner should always be "checking out" the possibility of moving into more directive interventions. Becoming more directive will likely be a step-by-step process with the child responding to the practitioner to engage in simple play activities (connecting sets) before moving into more skill or specific therapeutic interventions. Once the child is regularly participating in 15–20 minutes in connection set games, the practitioner can begin to implement more directive interventions that focus on specific skill development.

Teaching the Follow Me Approach to Parents

Parents should be taught how to conduct and have Follow Me play times at home with their child between sessions with the practitioner. It is advised that the practitioner conduct approximately 2–3 Follow Me Approach sessions with the child while the parents observe to make sure the parents understand how to do the Follow Me Approach correctly before the parents begin having Follow Me play times at home. The practitioner will have a 20–25 minute Follow Me session with the child (while the parents observe) and will use the remainder of the session time to process with parents, review the Follow Me session time, and answer questions the parents may have.

Practitioners will teach parents how to implement a Follow Me play time at home with their child. Practitioners will teach parents the core features of the Follow Me Approach, which include following the child's lead, making tracking and reflecting statements, asking questions, and attempting engagement with their child. Practitioners will also guide parents on how to implement the play times in the home setting. Parents should decide on a specific area in their home to have a Follow Me play time—preferably not the child's playroom or bedroom. Parents should also collect some toys to use during the Follow Me play time, and the toys should be boxed up and put away and only used for the Follow Me play times. Many children with autism spectrum disorder become territorial with their toys or rooms and do not welcome the parent trying to engage and initiate with them while they are playing with their toys or while they are in their own room. Children with ASD tend to have a strong "ownership" to their things and what they consider their space.

Many parents have found it beneficial to have the Follow Me play time in a different part of the home and to collect toys that are only used during the Follow Me play time. If a particular child is comfortable with this time occurring in his or her own room with his or her own toys, then that is perfectly acceptable. Some parents have discovered that the Follow Me play time occurs throughout the whole house with the child moving from room to room and the parent moving with the child. Any of these variations are acceptable as long as the parent is able to apply the core features of the Follow Me Approach. A list of toys and other materials that can be acquired is available in the Appendix. This list can be copied and given to parents. Practitioners should explain to parents that they do not need to acquire all the toys on the list. The list is a guide and parents should select just some of the toys that the parents believe will be the most engaging for their child.

Considerations When Teaching Parents the Follow Me Approach

1. The home setting may bring more challenges than the office setting. Be prepared for parent questions and to help parents find a way to work through home challenges and be successful with home Follow Me play times. The home play times may not look as structured or flow as smoothly as office sessions, but they can still be effective.
2. It is important to communicate to parents that they do not have to be 100 percent effective in their home play times. It will take some time and practice for parents to feel confident in understanding how to implement the approach. Parents may not be able to have a Follow Me play time every day. Parents should be encouraged to strive for as many play times as they can facilitate.
3. The length of the Follow Me Approach play time can be adapted in the home setting. For some children the Follow Me play time may start at 10 minutes a day with a goal of working up to 25 minutes. Some parents have found that they will have a 5–10 minute Follow Me time a couple of times a day. Again, variations are acceptable as long as parents are implementing the core features of the Follow Me approach.
4. Both parents can be involved in the Follow Me play time, but it is recommended that each parent have separate Follow Me play times with their child. A child with autism spectrum disorder may easily become overwhelmed from multiple people trying to engage with him or her or even multiple people in the room making tracking statements. Parents should have separate times; this benefits the parents as one parent does not become overwhelmed with being responsible for trying to implement a play time every day.
5. Other family members can be involved in implementing the Follow Me Approach. It is best if the practitioner can meet with the family member

who is going to have a Follow Me play time with the child and make sure that family member understands how to implement the approach. There are some important benefits to involving other family members. First, it provides support to the parent. Parents of children with ASD are usually doing a lot and having other family members be able to support with some of the tasks is extremely helpful to parents. Second, it helps generalize the child's connecting and relationship skills. The child can benefit from working with multiple people, not just one person.

6. Many parents discover, as they begin the Follow Me play times, that they start to generalize new ways of engaging and interacting with their child throughout the entire day. This generalization is not unusual as parents tend to find a new way of interacting with and understanding their child and discover an increase in relationship development with their child.

7. A parent guide is provided in the Appendix. The guide should be given to parents as a brief reminder of what to be doing during their home play times.

Limit Setting with the Follow Me Approach

During Follow Me sessions, limits are kept to a minimum. There may be times when a limit needs to be set either by the practitioner in the playroom or by parents in the home setting. Limits should consist of situations that would be dangerous for the child, for others, or situations where the child might be destroying property. If one of these situations arises, then the three Rs limit-setting model should be followed. The three Rs limit-setting model stands for redirect, replacement, and removal. (A guide for practitioners and parents is presented in the Appendix.)

Redirection: If the child begins to or is breaking a limit, the practitioner or parent should begin with redirection. The practitioner or parent would simply try to redirect the child to another activity, toy, or object to transition their attention off of the limit violation. There does not need to be any dialogue about a limit being broken or that the child needs to stop. The practitioner realizes the limit is being broken and moves to see if redirecting will suffice.

Replacement: If the child begins or is in process of breaking a limit, the practitioner or parent can begin with redirecting the child or begin with replacement. These two processes can be used interchangeably. Replacement means literally replacing what is happening with something new or different. If for example, the child is smashing a toy truck into the floor, which is breaking the truck, the practitioner or parent would quickly select another object, such as a rubber ball, and put it in the child's free hand while taking the truck away from the child. Replacement can also be replacing a game that is being played with the child with a different game. Where redirection is the act of transitioning the child's attention or trying to distract the child away, replacement is giving the child a tangible, acceptable alternative. As with redirecting, there does not need to be any dialogue about the limit being broken when using the replacement strategy.

Removal: If a child is beginning to or in the process of breaking a limit, redirecting and replacement should be implemented first. If these processes do not work, then removal is the final option. The first step in removal is verbally explaining to the child that they need to discontinue a behavior, or they may be removed from the room. If the verbal prompt does not stop the behavior, then removal is implemented. Removal is guiding the child into another location, possibly where the child can be alone or minimally supervised while the child calms. In an extreme case, removal might involve physically taking the child to a more secure location. If physical removal is necessary, then parents should be the person to physically remove the child. This is done in extreme cases where the child or others are in danger due to the child's behavior, and action is needed to keep everyone safe.

4 Research and Case Studies

Research

According to Parker & O'Brien (2011), the literature over many years abounds with case studies where changes in behavior are noted as a result of an intervention using play therapy. Various issues treated with play therapy approaches include learning disabilities, speech difficulties, anxiety issues, child abuse, trauma issues, family issues, and autism issues.

Multiple single-case-study designs have shown that children and adolescents that participate in AutPlay Therapy once a week for 6 months show skill gains in all three pre-assessed target areas of AutPlay Therapy: emotional regulation ability, social skills development, and connection (relationship development). Parent rating scales also support an increase in emotional regulation ability, social skills, and connection for children and adolescents who have participated in AutPlay Therapy once a week for 6 months. Parents also report gains in feeling more knowledgeable and empowered in their parenting abilities and less stress regarding their child's autism issues.

Although single case study designs continue to be done and continue to show gains for children with autism disorders, AutPlay Therapy would benefit from more controlled studies. More research across various practitioners is needed to scientifically validate AutPlay Therapy and show AutPlay Therapy as an evidence-based treatment approach for children and adolescents with ASD and other developmental disabilities. It is important to note that AutPlay Therapy influences are approaches rich in research that have shown success in treating children and adolescents with ASD and other developmental disabilities.

The National Professional Development Center (NPDC) on autism spectrum disorder and the National Standards Project (NSP) reviewed literature to establish evidence-based practices for individuals with autism spectrum disorder between the birth and age 22. Both reviews included literature up to and including 2007, and both applied rigorous criteria when determining which studies would be included as evidence of efficacy for a given practice. In 2014, the NPDC conducted an expanded and updated review, which yielded a total of 27 evidence-based practices.

AutPlay Therapy incorporates several of the approaches identified as evidence-based practices for treating children and adolescents with autism spectrum disorder. Practices incorporated into AutPlay Therapy procedures include cognitive behavioral intervention, modeling, naturalistic intervention, parent-implemented intervention, prompting, reinforcement, scripting, self-management, social narratives, social skills training, and visual supports. AutPlay Therapy, along with various other play-based treatments and play therapy approaches, has been shown to be a promising and emerging treatment for autism spectrum disorder and other developmental disabilities while incorporating several evidence-based practices. With further research gains, it is hopeful that AutPlay Therapy will continue be recognized through more randomized, controlled studies.

Case Studies

To date, several case studies and clinical outcomes have been conducted and recorded using AutPlay Therapy for children and adolescents with autism spectrum disorder, other neurodevelopmental disorders, and developmental disabilities. Each case study and clinical outcome reporting has indicated a significant improvement in targeted skill deficits in the core areas addresses by AutPlay Therapy. Four of the case studies are presented in an abbreviated version in this handbook.

Brian

Background

Brian, an 8-year-old male began AutPlay Therapy with a diagnosis of Autistic Disorder. Brian had been diagnosed as low functioning with limited conversation skills. Often, Brian would not make any verbalizations. When Brian did make verbalizations, he would mostly repeat others, sing a song he had heard, or mumble things to himself. A previous psychological evaluation using the Wechsler Nonverbal Scale of Ability scored Brian with a full-scale IQ score of 63.

Brian's mother completed the Autism Treatment Evaluation Checklist and the AutPlay Social Skills Inventory during the AutPlay intake assessment phase prior to therapy implementation to further define Brian's skill abilities and deficits. The practitioner conducted a formal child observation and a parent/child observation using the AutPlay observation forms. Through the parent completed inventories and practitioner observations, it was determined that the AutPlay Follow Me Approach would be the appropriate treatment intervention to begin with Brian and his mother. The Follow Me Approach was selected primarily due to Brian's low functioning ability and lack of attending and verbal skills. Treatment goals were established to address identified skill deficits (see Table 4.1).

Table 4.1 Parent Ratings before AutPlay Therapy Implementation (Brian)

Autism Treatment Evaluation Checklist	AutPlay Social Skills Inventory
• Asks meaningful questions = Not True • Prefers to be left alone = Very Descriptive • Avoids eye contact with others = Very Descriptive • Plays with toys appropriately = Not Descriptive	• Makes eye contact with others = 1 • Plays with others = 1 • Shares with others = 1 • Introduces self to others = 1 *Scale 1–5 (1 = not developed,* *5 = developed)*

Implementation of Approach

Sessions 1 through 3 focused on intake and assessment to establish treatment goals. Session 4 was the first Follow Me Approach. The practitioner met with Brian in a playroom and conducted a 25-minute Follow Me Approach session. Brian's mother observed the session via a monitor in another room. The remainder of the session time was used to follow up with Brian's mother about the Follow Me Approach and to begin teaching her how to have a Follow Me Approach at home with Brian. Sessions 5 through 7 followed the same format as Session 4. The practitioner conducted a 25-minute session using the Follow Me Approach and used the remainder of the session time to teach Brian's mother how to have the Follow Me play time at home. Session 8 continued with the practitioner having a 25-minute Follow Me Approach session with Brian and using the remainder of the time to conference with Brian's mother. At this point, Brian and his mother had begun to have Follow Me play times at home. Brian's mother reported that they had 5 Follow Me play times at home and that she was able to implement the approach with Brian for about 10 minutes before he began to become agitated.

By Session 9, Brian was beginning to interact with the practitioner more in session. Brian began to make eye contact, ask questions, answer about 40 percent of the practitioner's questions, and participate briefly in play with the practitioner. Brian's mother reported the same progress at home during home play times. Sessions 10 through 15 followed this pattern with Brian improving more in these areas in session with the practitioner and at home with his mother. In Session 16, the practitioner began to teach Brian's mother how to implement short, directive connection games to help move Brian toward a more directive intervention approach. Brian's mother was instructed to start with hitting a balloon back and forth with Brian and hiding a cotton ball on herself and letting Brian try to find it. In Session 17, Brian's mother reported that Brian started by hitting the balloon to her once and then walking away. By the time they returned for their therapy session, Brian was hitting the balloon back and forth with her on average seven times. She further reported that Brian started slowly participating in the cotton ball hiding game, but with continued implementation each play time, he had progressed in participating for about 5–7 minutes before losing interest.

In Sessions 18 through 23, Brian's mother continued to introduce connection games with Brian, and he continued to gain in cooperation. The practitioner also introduced the same connection games during therapy sessions, and Brian showed improvement in participating with the practitioner. Brian and his mother participated in 23 sessions over the course of 6 months; at which time, a postevaluation was conducted to assess if treatment goals were being met.

Outcome

At the end of 6 months, Brian and his mother had participated in 23 sessions with the practitioner. Brian's mother had implemented approximately 15 weeks of Follow Me plays times at home, approximately 4–5 times per week, with each play time lasting between 10–30 minutes. At the 23rd session mark, a postevaluation was conducted. Brian's mother completed the original inventories that she had previously completed during the intake and assessment phase of treatment. The Autism Treatment Evaluation Checklist and the AutPlay Social Skills Inventory were completed by Brian's mother and showed an improvement in every skill area that had originally been targeted as treatment goals for skill improvement. The practitioner also noted improvements in treatment goals and re-conducted a child observation and parent/child observation evaluation. Treatment goal improvements are noted in Table 4.2.

After 6 months of AutPlay Therapy intervention, each of Brian's originally targeted skill deficits showed significant improvement. The practitioner noted skill gains throughout the entire 6-month treatment period. Not only did parent ratings show a significant increase in each targeted skill area, but Brian's mother also reported a high degree of satisfaction with treatment results and reported feeling a greater connection with her son stating, "For the first time, I am experiencing fun interactive play time with him."

Table 4.2 Parent Ratings after 6 Months of AutPlay Therapy (Brian)

Autism Treatment Evaluation Checklist	*AutPlay Social Skills Inventory*
• Asks meaningful questions = Somewhat True • Prefers to be left alone = Somewhat Descriptive • Avoids eye contact with others = Not Descriptive • Plays with toys appropriately = Very Descriptive	• Makes eye contact with others = 4 • Plays with others = 3 • Shares with others = 3 • Introduces self to others = 3 *Scale 1–5 (1 = not developed, 5 = developed)*

Ethan

Background

Ethan, a 7-year-old male, began AutPlay Therapy with a diagnosis of autistic disorder, attention deficit hyperactivity disorder, and Down syndrome. Ethan had been diagnosed as low to moderate functioning. Ethan presented as a verbal child who seemed to possess adequate language development but often displayed echolalia. A previous psychological evaluation using the Wechsler Intelligence Scales for Children scored Ethan with a full-scale IQ score of 56. It was noted at the time of the evaluation that Ethan's participation was limited, thus effecting the outcome of the evaluation. This was possibly due to his autism or lack of attention, and his IQ was noted as likely being higher than his score indicated.

Ethan's father completed the Autism Treatment Evaluation Checklist, the AutPlay Social Skills Inventory, and the AutPlay Emotional Regulation Inventory during the AutPlay assessment phase prior to therapy implementation to further define Ethan's skill abilities and deficits. The practitioner conducted a formal child observation and a parent/child observation using the AutPlay observation forms. Through the parent completed inventories and practitioner observations, it was determined that Ethan and his father could begin the formal AutPlay Therapy process and treatment goals were established to address identified skill deficits (see Table 4.3).

Implementation of Approach

Sessions 1 through 3 focused on intake and assessment procedures to establish treatment goals. During the implementation of directive play intervention phase, Ethan and his father alternated sessions. Session 4 was a parent session. The practitioner and Ethan's father reviewed the treatment goals and discussed the first intervention that would be used with Ethan. The Me and My Feelings intervention (described in Chapter 5) was chosen to begin to work on emotional regulation-related goals. The intervention was explained to Ethan's father, and he was instructed to complete the intervention with Ethan at home

Table 4.3 Parent Ratings before AutPlay Therapy Implementation (Ethan)

Autism Treatment Evaluation Checklist	AutPlay Social Skills Inventory	AutPlay Emotional Regulation Inventory
• Explains what he/she wants = Not True • Asks meaningful questions = Not true • No eye contact = Very Descriptive	• Makes eye contact with others = 1 • Handles anger/frustration = 1 • Makes requests = 1 *Scale 1–5 (1 = not developed, 5 = developed)*	• My child can differentiate between at least 10 emotions = 1 • My child can state when he/she feels frustrated = 1 *Scale 1–5 (1 = not developed, 5 = developed)*

four times before their next session. Ethan's father was instructed not to start the intervention until Ethan had his session with the practitioner, so the practitioner could go over the intervention with Ethan. Session 5 was a child session with Ethan and the practitioner. The practitioner explained the Me and My Feelings intervention, and Ethan completed the intervention in session with the practitioner. Ethan was instructed that he and his father were going to complete the intervention at home four times before the next session. At the end of Session 5, the practitioner reminded Ethan's father that he would work with Ethan at home and complete the Me and My Feelings intervention four times and bring the completed results back to the next session.

Session 6 was a parent session. In this session, the practitioner reviewed the home assignment with Ethan's father. Ethan and his father had completed the Me and My Feelings intervention four times at home, and it seemed to go well. Ethan's father reported no problem with getting Ethan to complete the intervention, and he felt Ethan was able to understand some of his emotions better. He was instructed to complete three more Me and My Feelings interventions at home with Ethan before Ethan's session with the practitioner. The practitioner and Ethan's father also discussed the next intervention that would be taught to Ethan at his next session. Draw My Feeling Face (described in Chapter 5) was chosen as the next intervention to work on emotional regulation and social skill-related goals. Ethan's father was taught how to complete this intervention and instructed that he would start implementing it at home after Ethan's next session.

Sessions 7 through 20 followed the same format. Several directive play interventions were chosen to address treatment goals and Ethan's father was taught how to implement each one at home. Parent sessions focused on getting feedback from Ethan's father about how things were going with Ethan in general and how the home interventions were going, while child sessions focused on the practitioner implementing the interventions with Ethan. It is interesting to note that by Session 16 Ethan had stopped all echolalia at home and in sessions with the practitioner. Although eliminating the echolalia was not a direct treatment goal, it may have nonetheless been affected by working on Ethan's underlying issues.

In Session 21, by practitioner observations, Ethan was showing great gains toward his treatment goals. It was discussed with Ethan's father that they would have a couple more sessions and then re-evaluate Ethan in terms of his original treatment goals. In Session 24, Ethan's father completed updated inventories on Ethan (the same inventories he completed at the beginning of treatment), and in Sessions 24 and 25, the practitioner completed an updated child observation and parent/child observation using the AutPlay observation forms.

Outcome

At the end of 6 months, Ethan and his father had participated in 25 sessions with the practitioner. Ethan's father had implemented approximately 20 weeks of directive play interventions at home, ranging from daily implementation

Table 4.4 Parent Ratings after AutPlay Therapy Implementation (Ethan)

Autism Treatment Evaluation Checklist	AutPlay Social Skills Inventory	AutPlay Emotional Regulation Inventory
• Explains what he/she wants = Somewhat True • Asks meaningful questions = True • No eye contact = Not Descriptive	• Makes eye contact with others = 4 • Handles anger/ frustration = 3 • Makes requests = 5 *Scale 1–5 (1 = not developed, 5 = developed)*	• My child can differentiate between at least 10 emotions = 5 • My child can state when he/she feels frustrated = 5 *Scale 1–5 (1 = not developed, 5 = developed)*

to 3–4 times a week. At the 25th session mark, a postevaluation was conducted. Ethan's father completed the original inventories that he had previously completed during the intake and assessment phase of treatment: the Autism Treatment Evaluation Checklist, the AutPlay Social Skills Inventory, and the AutPlay Emotional Regulation Inventory, which showed an improvement in every skill area that was originally targeted as treatment goals for skill improvement. The practitioner also noted improvements in treatment goals and re-conducted a child observation and parent/child observation evaluation (see Table 4.4).

After 6 months of AutPlay Therapy intervention, each of Ethan's originally targeted skill deficits showed a significant improvement. The practitioner noted skill gains throughout the entire 6-month treatment period. Not only did parent ratings show a significant increase in each targeted skill areas, but Ethan's father also reported a high degree of satisfaction with treatment results, reported an overall improvement in Ethan's behavior with less behavior problems, and noted improvement in Ethan's speech and vocabulary. Although original treatment goals were satisfactorily met, during the re-evaluation, new treatment goals were established, and Ethan and his father continued to participate in therapy.

Eva

Background

Eva, a 9-year-old female, began AutPlay Therapy with a diagnosis of Asperger's syndrome, panic disorder with agoraphobia, and sensory processing disorder. Eva had been diagnosed as high functioning in regard to her autism spectrum disorder. Eva presented as a strong verbal child who seemed to possess above-average language development but significant sensory processing issues. A previous psychological evaluation using the Wechsler Intelligence Scales for Children scored Eva with a full-scale IQ score of 92.

Eva's parents completed the Autism Treatment Evaluation Checklist, the AutPlay Social Skills Inventory, and the AutPlay Emotional Regulation Inventory during the AutPlay intake and assessment phase prior to therapy

Table 4.5 Parent Ratings before AutPlay Therapy Implementation (Eva)

Autism Treatment Evaluation Checklist	AutPlay Social Skills Inventory	AutPlay Emotional Regulation Inventory
• Disagreeable/not compliant = Very Descriptive • Avoids contact with others = Very Descriptive • No eye contact = Very Descriptive • Tantrums = Very Descriptive • Anxious/fearful = Serious Problem	• Makes eye contact with others = 1 • Handles anger/ frustration = 1 • Introduces self to others = 1 *Scale 1–5 (1 = not developed, 5 = developed)*	• My child understands anxiety and can calm self when anxious = 1 • My child can state when he/she feels angry or anxious = 1 *Scale 1–5 (1 = not developed, 5 = developed)*

implementation to further define Eva's skill abilities and deficits. The practitioner conducted a formal child observation and a parent/child observation using the AutPlay observation forms. Through the parent-completed inventories and practitioner observations, it was determined that Eva and her parents could begin the formal AutPlay Therapy process. Treatment goals were established to address identified skill deficits (see Table 4.5).

Implementation of Approach

Sessions 1 through 3 focused on intake and assessment procedures designed to establish treatment goals. Eva and her parents alternated sessions with the practitioner. One week, Eva's parents would attend a session with the practitioner, and the next week Eva would attend a session with the practitioner. Session 4 was a parent session. The practitioner reviewed the treatment goals with Eva's parents and chose Draw My Feeling Face (described in Chapter 5) as the first intervention to use to help Eva with her identified skill deficits. Eva's parents were taught how to complete Draw My Feeling Face and instructed to implement the intervention at home five times between session times. Eva's parents were also instructed to wait to implement the intervention until Eva had her session with the practitioner. Session 5 was a child session. Eva met with the practitioner, the practitioner explained the Draw My Feeling Face intervention, and Eva and the practitioner completed the intervention during session time. Eva was given the instruction that she and her parents were going to play the intervention five times at home between sessions. At the end of Session 5, the practitioner reminded Eva's parents that they would now begin to implement the intervention at home and try to complete it five times before the next session.

Session 6 was a parent session. The practitioner reviewed with Eva's parents how the Draw My Feeling Face intervention went at home. Eva's parents reported that Eva participated well, and they had completed the intervention five times. They stated that Eva was able to go beyond the interventions and even talk about some of her negative feelings. The practitioner discussed with Eva's parents that the next intervention would be Feelings Detective (described in Chapter 5). The practitioner taught the intervention to Eva's parents, and they were again instructed to wait to implement the intervention until Eva had her session with the practitioner. In the meantime, the parents were instructed to complete four more Draw My Feeling Face interventions at home with Eva.

Session 7 was a child session. The practitioner reviewed with Eva how she felt the Draw My Feeling Face intervention went at home. Eva stated that she enjoyed playing the intervention with her parents. The practitioner discussed with Eva that they were going to do a new intervention called Feelings Detective. The practitioner taught the intervention to Eva, and they practiced the intervention during session time. Eva was instructed that she, with the help of her parents, would complete the Feelings Detective intervention at home before her next session. She was further instructed to bring the completed Feelings Detective sheet back with her to her next session with the practitioner. At the end of Session 7, the practitioner reminded Eva's parents that they would now be helping Eva complete the Feelings Detective intervention at home.

Sessions 8 through 22 progressed in the same format. Eva and her parents alternated sessions with the practitioner, and each time, a new intervention was introduced and taught to Eva and her parents to implement at home. Interventions were chosen based on the originally targeted treatment goals. The practitioner was continually noting when Eva seemed to display improvement toward an identified treatment goal. Parent session times also incorporated discussions regarding parenting strategies, forms of discipline, and school-related issues such as formulating an IEP and special education law.

In Session 22, by practitioner observations, Eva was showing great gains toward her treatment goals. It was discussed with Eva's parents that they would have a couple more sessions and then re-evaluate Eva in terms of her original treatment goals. In Session 24, Eva's parents completed updated inventories on Eva (the same inventories they completed at the beginning of treatment), and in Sessions 24 and 25, the practitioner completed an updated child observation and parent/child observation using the AutPlay observation forms.

Outcome

At the end of 6 months, Eva and her parents had participated in 25 sessions with the practitioner. Eva's parents had implemented approximately 20 weeks of directive play interventions at home, ranging from daily implementation to 3–4 times a week. At the 25th session mark, a postevaluation was conducted. Eva's parents completed the original inventories that they had previously completed during the intake and assessment phase of treatment: The Autism Treatment Evaluation Checklist, the AutPlay Social

Table 4.6 Parent Ratings after AutPlay Therapy Implementation (Eva)

Autism Treatment Evaluation Checklist	AutPlay Social Skills Inventory	AutPlay Emotional Regulation Inventory
• Disagreeable/not compliant = Somewhat Descriptive • Avoids contact with others = Not Descriptive • No eye contact = Not Descriptive • Tantrums = Somewhat Descriptive • Anxious/fearful = Minor Problem	• Makes eye contact with others = 5 • Handles anger/ frustration = 3 • Introduces self to others = 4 *Scale 1–5 (1 = not developed, 5 = developed)*	• My child understands anxiety and can calm self when anxious = 4 • My child can state when he/she feels angry or anxious = 5 *Scale 1–5 (1 = not developed, 5 = developed)*

Skills Inventory, and the AutPlay Emotional Regulation Inventory were completed and showed an improvement in every skill area that was originally targeted as treatment goals for skill improvement. The practitioner also noted improvements in treatment goals and re-conducted a child observation and parent/child observation evaluation. Treatment goal improvements are noted in Table 4.6.

After 6 months of AutPlay Therapy intervention, each of Eva's originally targeted skill deficits showed a significant improvement. The practitioner noted skill gains throughout the entire 6-month treatment period. Not only did parent ratings show a significant increase in each targeted skill areas, but Eva's parents also reported an overall improvement in Eva's behavior with less behavior problems and less tantrums. They further reported improvement with Eva's sensory processing issues. Although original treatment goals were satisfactorily met, during the re-evaluation, new treatment goals were established, and Eva and her parents continued to participate in therapy.

Logan

Background

Logan, a 15-year-old male, began AutPlay Therapy with a diagnosis of Asperger's syndrome and fragile X syndrome. Logan had been diagnosed as moderate to high functioning with poor social skills. Logan had just begun attending public school after being in a private autism school. A previous psychological evaluation using the Wechsler Intelligence Scales for Children scored Logan with a full-scale IQ score of 93.

Logan's mother completed the Autism Treatment Evaluation Checklist and the AutPlay Social Skills Inventory during the AutPlay intake and assessment phase prior to therapy implementation to further define Logan's skill abilities and deficits. The practitioner conducted a formal child observation and a parent/child observation using the AutPlay observation forms.

Table 4.7 Parent Ratings before AutPlay Therapy Implementation (Logan)

Autism Treatment Evaluation Checklist	AutPlay Social Skills Inventory
• Lacks friends/companions = Very Descriptive • Insensitive to other's feelings = Very Descriptive • Hyperactive = Serious Problem • Obsessive speech = Serious Problem • Rigid routines = Serious Problem	• Listens without interrupting = 1 • Knows how to join a group = 1 • Makes friends with others = 1 • Ignores distractions = 1 • Understands manners = 1 *Scale 1–5 (1 = not developed,* *5 = developed)*

Through the parent-completed inventories and practitioner observations, it was determined that Logan and his mother could begin the formal AutPlay Therapy process. Treatment goals were established to address identified skill deficits (see Table 4.7).

Implementation of Approach

Sessions 1 through 3 focused on intake and assessment to better identify Logan's skill strengths and deficits. Logan and his mother participated in weekly sessions together. Session 4 focused on going over treatment goals with Logan and his mother and identifying the first AutPlay intervention to implement. Social Skills Cross-Off (described in Chapter 6) was chosen to help address Logan's treatment goals. The practitioner worked with Logan and his mother to establish specific social skills to use in the game. The practitioner, Logan, and his mother played the game together during their session time. Logan and his mother were instructed to play Social Skills Cross-Off at home 3–4 times before their next session. Session 5 began by discussing with Logan and his mother how the home intervention went. They both stated the intervention went well; Logan practiced some useful social skills, and the interaction between Logan and his mother during the intervention was positive. The practitioner discussed with Logan and his mother that they were going to learn a new intervention. Action Identification (described in Chapter 6) was chosen to further address social skill-related deficits. The practitioner, Logan, and his mother played the intervention during their session time, and Logan and his mother were instructed to complete the intervention four times before their next session.

Sessions 6 through 22 followed the same format. At each session, an AutPlay intervention was chosen to address Logan's treatment goals, and Logan and his mother participated by practicing the intervention during their session time. Logan and his mother were taught the intervention and given instructions for implementing the intervention at home between sessions. There were a few sessions where the same intervention was repeated and implemented for two weeks in a row.

In Session 22, by practitioner observations, Logan was showing significant progress toward his treatment goals. It was discussed with Logan and his

Table 4.8 Parent Ratings after AutPlay Therapy Implementation (Logan)

Autism Treatment Evaluation Checklist	AutPlay Social Skills Inventory
• Lacks friends/companions = Somewhat Descriptive • Insensitive to other's feelings = Not Descriptive • Hyperactive = Minor Problem • Obsessive speech = Minor Problem • Rigid routines = Minor Problem	• Listens without interrupting = 5 • Knows how to join a group = 3 • Makes friends with others = 3 • Ignores distractions = 4 • Understands manners = 4 *Scale 1–5 (1 = not developed, 5 = developed)*

mother that they would have a couple more sessions then re-evaluate Logan in terms of his original treatment goals. In Session 24, Logan's mother completed updated inventories on Logan (the same inventories she completed at the beginning of treatment), and in Sessions 24 and 25, the practitioner completed an updated child observation and parent/child observation using the AutPlay observation forms.

Outcome

At the end of 6 months, Logan and his mother had participated in 25 sessions with the practitioner. Logan and his mother had implemented approximately 20 weeks of directive play interventions at home, ranging from daily implementation to 3–4 times a week. At Session 24, a postevaluation was conducted. Logan's mother completed the original inventories that she had previously completed during the intake and assessment phase of treatment: The Autism Treatment Evaluation Checklist and the AutPlay Social Skills Inventory were completed and showed an improvement in every skill area that was originally targeted as treatment goals for skill improvement. The practitioner also noted improvements in treatment goals and re-conducted a child observation and parent/child observation evaluation. Treatment goal improvements are noted in Table 4.8.

After 6 months of AutPlay Therapy intervention, each of Logan's originally targeted skill deficits showed a significant improvement. The practitioner noted skill gains throughout the entire 6-month treatment period. Not only did parent ratings show a significant increase in each targeted skill areas, but Logan's mother also reported significant improvements in school behavior and social involvement at school. Logan further reported feeling more confident being around peers and more success with making friends, especially at school. Although original treatment goals were satisfactorily met, during the re-evaluation new treatment goals were established, and Logan and his mother continued to participate in therapy.

5 Emotional Regulation Interventions

Feeling Face Fans

Primary Target Area	Emotional Regulation
Secondary Target Areas	Anxiety Reduction, Social Skills, Connection
Level	Child and Adolescent
Materials	White Paper or Paper Plates, Wood Sticks, Glue, Markers
Modality	Individual

Introduction

Children and adolescents with ASD often have a difficult time regulating their emotions, which includes identifying emotions and connecting feelings to real-life situations. This intervention creates a strong visual aid that the child can keep to help him or her identify emotions and connect his or her emotions to applicable experiences.

Instructions

The child is instructed to cut 2 round circles (or any shape) out of white pieces of paper. (White paper plates can also be used.) On each of the 2 circles, the child draws a feeling face and then writes the feeling words on the pieces of paper that correspond with the feeling face. The practitioner should instruct the child to try and think of opposite feelings like mad and happy. The child glues both sides together with a wooden stick in the middle. The child can make several Feeling Face Fans representing several different opposite feelings. The practitioner and child talk about the feelings the child has chosen and the concept of opposite feelings. The practitioner and child practice making faces that match the feeling faces the child drew initially and talk about a time or situation when the child has experienced the feeling. If the child is having a difficult time thinking of an experience, the practitioner can ask some helpful questions like "What do you feel in school during PE class?" or "How does your brother make you feel?" These types of questions may help the child connect the emotion with a real experience.

Rationale

This technique helps the child work on identifying, understanding, and expressing emotions (especially the concept of opposite emotions and connecting emotions to real experiences). This technique also works on understanding body language and recognizing emotions in others. The child may have difficulty identifying feelings and identifying opposites. The practitioner should work with the child to identify feelings and make the Feeling Face Fans; the more impairment that a child has, the more directive and instructive the practitioner will be.

Feeling Face Fans

Me and My Feelings

Primary Target Area	Emotional Regulation
Secondary Target Area	Anxiety Reduction
Level	Child and Adolescent
Materials	White Paper, Construction Paper, Markers, Scissors, Glue
Modality	Individual, Group

Introduction

Me and My Feelings is designed to help children and adolescents identify and make a connection with the emotions that they experience. It incorporates a strong visual element to help the child recognize his or her emotional self and begin to talk about and process his or her emotions.

Instructions

The practitioner explains to the child that they will be working on identifying emotions. The child draws an outline of a person on a white piece of paper. The child makes the person look like him- or herself (face, hair, etc.). Using construction paper, the child cuts out different colors to represent different feelings the child has felt. The construction paper should be cut in different sizes to represent different levels of feelings; small pieces are feelings that are not felt as often, while larger pieces are feelings the child has more often. The child glues the pieces on his or her paper person, placing them wherever he or she wants. The child then writes the feeling on the piece of construction paper that he or she has glued onto his or her person. The practitioner discusses with the child the feelings that he or she selected and talks about situations or experiences when he or she has felt that way.

Rationale

Me and My Feelings helps children and adolescents work on identifying, understanding, and expressing emotions. The child also works on fine motor skills and verbal communication with this technique. The child's feelings may change day-to-day, and the level that the child is feeling will also change from day-to-day. This is a concept that can be discussed with the child along with helping the child understand that all people experience various emotions at different times. Parents can be taught to implement this intervention at home with their child and can be encouraged to complete a Me and My Feelings person periodically to help their child gain more practice in identifying and discussing emotions.

Me and My Feelings

Feelings Scenarios

Primary Target Area	Emotional Regulation
Secondary Target Areas	Social Skills, Behavior Change
Level	Child and Adolescent
Materials	Index Cards, Pencil
Modality	Individual

Introduction

Children and adolescents with ASD and other developmental disorders often struggle with appropriately expressing their emotions. This intervention helps children and adolescents make a connection between emotions they may experience, specific scenarios that trigger those emotions, and how to appropriate express their emotions. This intervention can be tailored to cover real-life scenarios that the child has struggled with in the past.

Instructions

Before the session, the practitioner writes down different situations or scenarios that would evoke different feelings. (Typically, the practitioner will write down, on index cards, situations the child has struggled with in the past.) The practitioner should try to think of situations that would be relevant for the specific child. The practitioner and child take turns reading the situations and showing what feeling(s) would be appropriate in the situation using only body language and facial expression. Once the feeling(s) has been shown with body language, the practitioner and child can discuss the feeling(s) appropriate for the situation and discuss if the child has ever been in that situation and felt that way. The practitioner can further discuss with the child ideas for how to appropriately express the emotions that he or she is feeling in the situation. Once all of the situations have been completed, the practitioner can ask the child if he or she has any scenarios they would like to practice.

Rationale

This technique helps develop identifying and expressing emotions, recognizing emotions in others, and understanding emotion/situation recognition. This technique also works on understanding body language. This is an effective technique to practice specific situations that are difficult for the child to handle in terms of his or her emotional management. If the child is capable, a further process question would be to ask the child what he or she could do to manage his or her emotions better in the situation. Parents can be taught this intervention and continue to practice with their child at home.

Feelings Scenarios Examples

A student at your school tells you that you are stupid.

You are playing your favorite video game, and your mom tells you that you have to stop and go to the grocery store with her.

Your mom and dad tell you that you are going on a trip to Disney World.

Your sister breaks your favorite toy.

You win an award at school for best behavior.

You have an excellent school report card.

You are playing at home and accidently break one of your parent's pictures.

You are at the mall with your parents and get lost from them.

Your teacher gives you a surprise math test, and you do not know how to do it.

When you get home from school, you want to play on your computer but discover it is broken.

Your dad tells you that you have to go watch a school play that your brother is participating in.

Your teacher tells you that you will not have any homework for a whole week.

You are playing at recess, and some other students ask you to play with them.

You are playing at recess, and no one else will play with you.

You are riding in your car, and your brother and sister are being extremely loud.

Some other students at school start making fun of you.

Your parents buy you a present that is your favorite new toy.

Feelings Detective

Primary Target Area	Emotional Regulation
Secondary Target Area	Social Skills
Level	Child and Adolescent
Materials	Paper, Pencil
Modality	Individual, Group

Introduction

Children and adolescents with ASD not only have challenges in recognizing their own emotions but often have a difficult time recognizing emotions in others. This intervention helps children and adolescents learn to identify emotions in others and in themselves. It also helps children learn to focus on and pay attention to other people.

Instructions

The practitioner will type or write on a piece of paper a list of feelings the child must find during the week (an example is included here). The practitioner explains to the child that he or she will be the practitioner's Feelings Detective, and the child is to take the list home to observe people to identify each feeling on the list. If the child thinks he or she observes a person displaying one of the feelings, he or she must verify that with the person showing the feeling or with his or her parent. The child writes down the person and situation where he or she found the feeling. The child brings the list back to the next session, and the practitioner and child go over the list together and talk about the feelings that the child found. This is usually followed by creating another feelings list and sending it home, this time with the instructions that the child has to find the feelings in him- or herself. When he or she notices that he or she is feeling the emotion, the situation should be written down on the feeling list paper, and the child is instructed to bring the list back to the next counseling session to discuss with the practitioner.

Rationale

Feelings Detective works on identifying and recognizing emotions in others. This technique also works on the social skills areas of observing others body language and paying attention to what others are saying. The practitioner should create a list of basic feelings to begin with such as happy, sad, mad, etc. More lists can be created at a later session with more advanced feelings. Parents should be instructed to assist their child in completing the list by helping the child verify feelings and by providing opportunities for the child to observe other people.

Feelings Detective Worksheet

Name: _____

Happy

Lonely

Excited

Mad

Proud

Nervous

Loved

Shy

Jealous

An Emotional Story

Primary Target Area	Emotional Regulation
Secondary Target Area	Anxiety Reduction
Level	Child and Adolescent
Materials	Paper, Pencil
Modality	Individual, Group

Introduction

Children and adolescents with an ASD often have low receptive language ability. This intervention helps children work on focusing and listening for key words or phrases especially related to emotions. It also helps children recognize when someone is experiencing an emotion and why another person might be experiencing a certain emotion.

Instructions

Before the session, the practitioner writes 1–3 short stories that reference people feeling various emotions (some examples are included here). The practitioner reads one of the emotional stories to the child. As the practitioner is reading the story, the child is instructed to listen, stop the practitioner, and identify every time an emotion is expressed in the story. The child must state what emotion is expressed, who in the story is expressing the emotion, why the person in the story is expressing the emotion, and if he or she would feel that way in the same situation. These are questions that can be asked by the practitioner each time the child stops the story to identify an emotion. After the story is finished, the practitioner can read another story or ask the child if he or she wants to write his or her own emotional story. If the child writes his or her own emotional story, he or she can then read the story and have the practitioner identify the emotions. When reading the story to the child, it is likely the child will miss some emotions. The practitioner should stop the story and mention to the child that there was an emotion that the child missed and re-read that section of the story to provide the child an opportunity to identify the missed emotion.

Rationale

This technique works on sharing emotional experiences as well as several other emotional regulation categories. The difficulty and length of the story should vary depending on the child's age and functioning level. Several different stories can be written referencing many different situations in the child's life. Children who struggle to recognize the emotions in the story may need to start by reading the story themselves, circling all the emotions they find in the story, then discussing the emotions.

Emotional Story Example 1: Sam's First Day of School

Sam was awakened by his alarm clock. It was 7:00am and time to get up and get ready for the first day of school. Sam was feeling tired and really didn't want to get out of bed. Sam's mother told him he had to get out of bed and get dressed; she was worried he would miss the school bus. Sam got out of bed and started getting dressed. Sam was excited to see some friends he had not seen all summer but anxious that there might be a bully at school. Sam got dressed and ate his breakfast, which gave him a sick feeling in his stomach. Sam continued to feel anxious as he got on the school bus. There was a lot of noise on the bus, and Sam was getting irritated by all the loudness. The bus finally got to school, and Sam went into his classroom. Sam was feeling relieved to finally be at school. Sally, one of Sam's best friends, came and sat beside him; this made Sam happy, and he thought maybe school was not so bad. Sam actually started to feel excited about going to school this year even if it meant he had to get up at 7:00am every morning.

Emotional Story Example 2: Sally's Brother

Sally walked into her room ready to play with all her toys and have a lot of fun! As she walked into her room, her mood changed from excited to angry! Sally's little brother Michael was in her room, and he had broken several of her toys. Sally was so angry that she yelled at the top of her lungs for Michael to get out of her room. Michael seemed surprised and scared at the same time. Michael quickly ran out of Sally's room. As Sally looked around her room, she felt sad; many of her favorite toys were broken. Sally's mother heard Sally yell at Michael and came into Sally's room. She saw Sally looking sad and upset and realized what had happened. Sally's mother told Sally that everything would be OK; they would replace all the toys that had gotten broken. Sally started to feel happy. Sally's mother also told Sally that they would get a special lock for her door so her brother could not get in. Sally was excited to get some new toys and relieved that her brother would not be able to get in her room.

Alphabet Feelings

Primary Target Area	Emotional Regulation
Secondary Target Area	Social Skills
Level	Child and Adolescent
Materials	Alphabet Feeling List, Feeling Face Cards/Pictures
Modality	Individual

Introduction

Children and adolescents with autism spectrum disorder often need to work on a variety of skills related to emotional regulation. This intervention covers identifying emotions, recognizing emotions in others, talking about emotion producing situations, and how to handle negative emotions. It also incorporates social skill practice in body language and noticing others, specifically in regard to emotional expression.

Instructions

The practitioner explains to the child that they will be talking about feelings using the letters of the alphabet. The practitioner instructs the child to pick one letter from the alphabet and turn it into a feeling word such as A for "Angry" (see example chart included here). If needed, the practitioner can help the child identify a feeling. The practitioner then shows a picture of someone expressing that feeling. (Pictures can be cut out from a magazine or presented from a deck of feeling face cards.) The practitioner asks the child to show with his or her face and body what the feeling looks like, then asks the child to think of a time when he or she has felt that way, and finally how he or she expressed the feeling. If it is a negative feeling, the child is asked to try and identify something that helps him or her feel better. After the feeling has been completed, the practitioner and child can pick another letter and complete the process with another feeling.

Rationale

Alphabet Feelings is an intervention that focuses on the full range of emotional regulation skills. This technique helps work on overall managing of emotions as well as several other emotional regulation categories. Depending on the functioning level of the child, the practitioner may do a great deal of instructing in this technique. This intervention is also easily adapted to address whatever components the practitioner wants to work on with the child. This technique can be completed multiple times using all the letters of the alphabet and identifying multiple feelings for each letter. Parents can be taught how to implement this intervention at home and work on completing the entire alphabet addressing a variety of different feelings.

Alphabet Feelings

A angry, annoyed, amused, anxious, awkward, abandoned, afraid, affectionate, aggressive, arrogant, admired, adventurous, ashamed
B brave, bold, blissful, bitter, bored, battered
C calm, caring, cheerful, confident, confused, comfortable, cooperative, curious, considerate, combative
D defiant, discouraged, disappointed, dedicated, dejected, daring, delighted, depressed, devoted, dumb, distracted, different, destructive
E excited, enraged, envious, energetic, encouraged, eager, ecstatic, embarrassed, empty, excluded, enthusiastic
F fearful, fearless, frightened, free, fierce, fragile, fun, funny, furious, frustrated, frail, friendly
G genuine, glad, grateful, guilty
H happy, hateful, healthy, helpless, honest, hopeless, hopeful, horrible, hostile, humiliated, hurt
I impatient, inconsiderate, insecure, inspired, insulted, interested, intense, intrigued, irritated, isolated
J jealous, joyful
K kind
L lonely, loving, loved, lousy, lovely, livid
M mad, mean, miserable, moody, mournful, manic, malicious
N nice, nasty, needy, nervous, negative, neglected
O optimistic, outraged, overjoyed, overwhelmed
P peaceful, proud, panicked, patient, pathetic, peaceful, pessimistic, pleased, polite
Q quiet
R rejected, rebellious, rage, regretful, rejected, relieved, rotten, ruined, resentful
S sad, satisfied, scared, secure, sensitive, shy, spontaneous, strong, surprised, sweet, sympathetic, stressed, sleepy, smart, stupid
T terrified, terrific, tender, tense, thoughtful, threatened, thrilled, tough, trustworthy, tired
U uncomfortable, understanding, unappreciated, uncertain, unloved, unworthy, useless, unusual
V vulnerable, violent, violated, vivacious
W weird, weak, warm, wild, worried, worthless, worthy
X (can you think of a feeling)?
Y young, youthful, yucky
Z zany, zealous

Worry Tree

Primary Target Area	Emotional Regulation
Secondary Target Area	Anxiety Reduction
Level	Child and Adolescent
Materials	Construction Paper, Markers, Scissors, Glue
Modality	Individual, Group

Introduction

Children and adolescents with ASD and other developmental disorders tend to be strong visual learners. Worry Tree creates a visual aid that children can keep at home to help them remember approaches to self-calm and decrease their worry and anxiety.

Instructions

The practitioner tells the child they will be working on ways to help the child calm and regulate when he or she is feeling anxiety and dysregulated. The practitioner instructs the child to draw a tree on a piece of construction paper. The child then makes several leaves out of construction paper and tapes them on the tree. The practitioner and child write different things the child worries about on the leaves. The practitioner and child talk about the different worries and if each worry is a legitimate thing to worry about or something that is not realistic. (This is a good time to talk about realistic versus unrealistic worries, as children with ASD can have several unrealistic or irrational worries.) The practitioner and child then talk about a calming technique that can be done for each worry. The calming techniques are then written anywhere on the tree. The practitioner and child role-play through scenarios that create anxiety and practice a calming strategy. The child takes the tree home and is encouraged to reference it to help him or her remember the calming techniques when he or she feels worried. If the child discovers that there is something on a leaf that he or she no longer worries about, then he or she can remove that leaf from the tree, and he or she can also add leaves if he or she discovers something new that creates anxiety.

Rationale

This technique helps children and adolescents work on understanding, expressing, and managing emotions, especially negative emotions of worry and anxiety. The tree can be modified to represent any emotion the child needs to work on such as an angry tree or a scared tree. The functioning level of the child will dictate how much of this technique the practitioner helps with in terms of identifying situations that create the emotion and identifying the calming techniques to help control the emotion. Fine motor skills and verbal communication skills are also addressed in this intervention.

Worry Tree

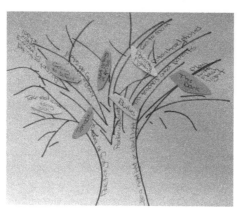

Schedule Party

Primary Target Area	Emotional Regulation
Secondary Target Areas	Anxiety Reduction, Behavior Change
Level	Child
Materials	Various Party Toys, Schedule Materials
Modality	Individual

Introduction

Children with ASD are typically strong visual learners, and they often use and benefit from a variety of visual schedules. One type of visual schedule that is helpful for regulation and staying calm during transitions is a weekly visual schedule. This intervention describes a playful and engaging way to create a weekly visual schedule for children with ASD.

Instructions

The practitioner works with the parents to teach them how to create a visual schedule displaying the child's weekly activities. There are a variety of ways to present the schedule, and parents should choose the method they feel will work best. A dry erase board works well, but other examples would be a paper schedule, one made with a computer program, one displayed on the child's tablet, or a Velcro schedule. The practitioner teaches the parents how to have a "Schedule Party." Parents should establish a time each week to go over the next week's schedule and have the child participate. This should be called a "Schedule Party," and the parents should have party hats to wear, noisemakers, balloons, etc. Parent and child should go through each day and after each day has been scheduled, the child should get a piece of candy, get to blow a noisemaker, get to hit some balloons, etc. The idea is to have a small celebration after each day has been scheduled. The parents are encouraged to keep the atmosphere fun and engaging for the child. Weekly schedules typically include each day of the week, and each day is broken down hourly from the time the child wakes to when he or she goes to sleep.

Rationale

This technique helps children work on general regulation and feeling positive and comfortable with the use of a weekly visual schedule. The Schedule Party presents the opportunity for the parent and child to have a playful interaction and for the child to feel positively about his or her visual schedule. Visual schedules in general are helpful for decreasing dysregulation and helping children transition. The format of the schedule will depend on the child's ability and developmental level (words versus pictures). For more information on creating various visual schedules, visit www.handsinautism.org. Several weekly visual schedule examples can also be found online by searching for visual schedule examples.

Same Plan/New Plan

Primary Target Area	Emotional Regulation
Secondary Target Areas	Anxiety Reduction, Behavior Change
Level	Child
Materials	Foam or Card Board Pieces, Markers, Art Decorations, Glue
Modality	Individual

Introduction

Children with ASD and developmental disorders often have a difficult time with transitions, spontaneous happenings, and changes to the original plan the child was expecting. This intervention provides parents with a prop to help children handle changes to the plan or schedule and produce a more calm and regulated response from the child.

Instructions

Using card stock or foam pieces, the practitioner and child will create 2 cards. One card will have a large "S" drawn on it, and the other will have a large "N" drawn on it. The child will decorate both cards. The practitioner will talk about how sometimes there is a plan and something happens and it changes (the N card) and sometimes the plan stays the same (the S card). The child will take the cards home and give them to the parents. The parents will use the cards to help the child understand when there is a new plan. The child and parents are both instructed that the parents will keep the cards, and when there is a new plan, the parents will present the N card to the child and wait a few seconds to let the child process that he or she is about to hear a new plan. Then, the parents will tell the child what the new plan is. The S card is used when the child asks if there is a new plan or if things are the same. The parent can present the S card to the child if the plan is the same.

Rationale

This technique helps children with managing emotions in regard to transitions and spontaneous or unplanned changes. The practitioner should emphasize to the child that the N card represents a new plan and the S card represents the same plan. It is important that the child understand when he or she gets the N card that a new plan, different from what the child was expecting, is about to be presented and that this will be OK. This helps the child make an association that it is OK to hear a change and begin to prepare themselves. Parents are taught the approach so they know what the cards are for when the child brings them home. Parents may want to make more than one set of cards so they keep one in their car and one at home.

Same Plan/New Plan Cards

Mr. Potato Head Feelings

Primary Target Area	Emotional Regulation
Secondary Target Areas	Social Skills, Connection
Level	Child
Materials	Mr. and Mrs. Potato Head Toys
Modality	Individual, Family, Group

Introduction

Children and adolescents with autism spectrum disorder and developmental disorders often struggle with identifying emotions. This intervention creates a playful way to engage children in identifying facial expression of emotion. Several different emotion expressions can be made with Mr. Potato Head accessory pieces. It is best for the practitioner and child to both have a Mr. Potato Head so both can make feeling faces that the other has to try and identify.

Instructions

Using a Mr. or Mrs. Potato Head (Hasbro Toys) and various accessory pieces, the child will create as many potato head faces as he or she can showing as many feeling faces as he or she can think of to create. The practitioner also participates and creates Mr. Potato Head Feeling Faces. Once a face has been created, it is shown to the other person, and the other person has to try and identify the feeling face. Once the correct feeling has been identified, the child and practitioner try to make the feeling expression on their own faces. The practitioner can also ask the child to share about a time that he or she has felt that way. The practitioner and child should try to create as many Mr. Potato Head Feeling Faces as they can think of. It is helpful if the practitioner has collected several accessory pieces.

Rationale

Mr. Potato Head Feelings works on identifying, understanding, and expressing emotions. It also works on fine motor skills and social skills related to body language and facial recognition. The practitioner will need to purchase a Mr. or Mrs. Potato Head; the more accessory pieces, the more options in creating the feeling faces. Mr. Potato Head Feelings is a positive and playful way to engage children through a popular toy. This intervention can be implemented in a group setting and taught to parents to implement at home with the whole family participating and playing with the child.

Mr. Potato Head Feelings

What Are They Feeling?

Primary Target Area	Emotional Regulation
Secondary Target Area	Social Skills
Level	Child and Adolescent
Materials	Magazines, Index Cards, Pen, Glue
Modality	Individual, Group

Introduction

Children and adolescents with ASD and other developmental disorders often have a difficult time recognizing and understanding emotions in other people. This intervention helps children think about and identify what another person might be feeling and why they might be feeling that way.

Instructions

Using magazines, the child is instructed to cut out pictures of people showing different emotions. Once the child has gathered several different examples, the child glues the pictures on index cards and writes on the pictures the emotion the person is showing. On the back of the index card, the child writes all the things that he or she believes could make the person feel that way. If the emotion identified is a negative one, an additional question for the child might be "What would help that person feel better?" Instead of making the cards from magazines, practitioners may want to buy cards that display people in different situations showing different emotions. These cards can usually be found at education supply stores. Depending on the child's emotional regulation ability, he or she may need help in identifying emotions and labeling them correctly. The child may also need help in thinking of reasons a person may be feeling the emotion. The practitioner should guide and help the child through each step of this intervention, taking advantage of opportunities to help teach the child about emotions.

Rationale

This technique helps children and adolescents work on identifying, understanding, and expressing emotions and recognizing emotions in others. Children also work on fine motor skills and verbal communication with this technique. Children and adolescents can create a whole deck of different feelings and reasons why someone would feel the emotions. Children can also be continually adding to their deck; when a child identifies a new feeling, he or she can create a new card and add it to his or her card deck. These cards should be created and sent home with the child. The child can use the card deck to reference emotions he or she might identify in him- or herself or emotions identified in other people. Parents can also be taught to create new cards at home with their child.

What Are They Feeling?

- Got some good news
- Gets to go to her favorite place and is excited
- Dancing
- Playing and having fun

- Other kids did not want to play with him.
- Lost the soccer game
- Got hurt playing soccer
- Someone teased him

Feelings Swatch

Primary Target Area	Emotional Regulation
Secondary Target Areas	Anxiety Reduction, Behavior Change
Level	Child and Adolescent
Materials	Paint Chips, Hole Punch, Markers, Key Ring
Modality	Individual, Family, Group

Introduction

Often children with autism spectrum disorder struggle to communicate to others what they are feeling, especially when they are very dysregulated. This intervention provides children and adolescents with a tool they can use to help communicate what they are feeling and gives adults a better understanding of what is happening with the child.

Instructions

The practitioner explains to the child that they are going to use paint sample swatches to make a Feelings Swatch key ring. The practitioner gives the child several paint chip samples that have been cut into smaller sizes. There should be a variety of colors available for the child to choose from. The child thinks of different feelings that he or she experiences sometimes and chooses a paint chip color to go with each feeling. The child writes the feelings on the paint chips. Once all the paint chips are completed, the child uses a hole punch on each chip and then places the chips on a key ring. The child has created a Feelings Swatch key ring that he or she can carry around and use to show others what he or she is feeling. Once the Feelings Swatch is complete, the practitioner and child review each feeling together and talk about times the child has felt each feeling. The practitioner and child can also practice scenarios where the child might use his or her key ring. It is recommended to begin with 8–10 feelings. More feelings can be added at any time. The practitioner will want to make sure that feelings the child typically struggles with are included on the key ring.

Rationale

This technique helps work on identifying, understanding, and managing emotions. This technique represents a great assistive technology device that the child can use at home or school to help communicate to others what he or she is feeling. The child can add feelings any time. When creating the feelings swatch, it will likely be necessary for the practitioner to add some feelings that the child leaves out. It is important to make sure that feelings the child often has are represented on the swatch. Parents are taught about the swatch and instructed to encourage their child to use the swatch. Parents can also help the child add feelings to the swatch.

Feelings Swatch

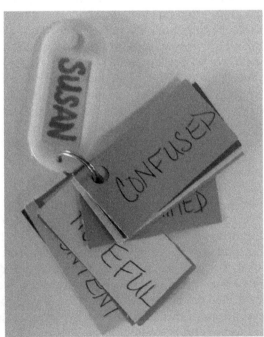

Feeling Face Cards

Primary Target Area	Emotional Regulation
Secondary Target Areas	Social Skills, Connection
Level	Child and Adolescent
Materials	Deck of Feeling Face Cards
Modality	Individual, Family, Group

Introduction

Using a deck of feeling face cards (which can be purchased from several education and therapy stores), the practitioner and child will play various popular card games with an emotion-focused twist. Example games might include Feelings Go Fish, Feelings Memory, or Feelings Bingo.

Instructions

Feelings Bingo is played by separating all the feeling matching cards into 2 piles. From one pile, lay 2 rows of 5 cards face up so each player has 2 rows of 5 cards. (This creates the "bingo card" showing the feeling faces the player is trying to match.) Take the remaining cards and shuffle them in with the other pile. Place the pile down between the players, each player draws a card and tries to find a match. All the matches have to be drawn for someone to win. Each time there is a match, that person has to share the definition of the feeling.

In Feelings Go Fish and Feelings Memory, each time a match is found, the person has to share a time that he or she has felt that way. All three of these games can have multiple variations, and multiple games can be created with a deck of feeling face cards. The practitioner may develop several ways to add an emotion skill focus to other popular card games. The *Feelings Playing Cards* by Jim Borgman contain instructions for several popular card games that can be adapted to address emotional regulation skills.

Rationale

The Feeling Face Cards intervention works on all of the emotional regulation categories depending on the variation of the games. The practitioner will want to consider the functioning level of the child when selecting a card game. Parents can easily be taught the games and are encouraged to purchase a deck of feeling face cards and periodically play the card games with their child. This intervention provides an opportunity for the whole family to participate. Several different games can be played, and the games can be played repeatedly.

Theory of Mind (ToM) Puppets

Primary Target Area	Emotional Regulation
Secondary Target Area	Social Skills
Level	Child
Materials	Puppets
Modality	Individual

Introduction

This intervention works on helping children learn theory of mind (ToM), which is defined as the ability to understand that others can have beliefs, desires, and intentions that are different from our own. Theory of mind is often lacking in children with ASD, and this skill deficit can create emotional and social difficulties.

Instructions

The practitioner explains to the child that they will be using puppets to talk about how people have different opinions and can feel differently about the same thing. This technique uses puppets to help teach theory of mind to children, but miniature people could also be used. The practitioner chooses 3 puppets (people puppets are preferable) and creates a simple story. Each puppet has a different thought and feeling about the same thing. For example, each puppet tastes an apple pie: One puppet loves it, one puppet hates it, and one puppet says the pie is OK. Then the puppets taste a different kind of pie, such as a chocolate, and again, each one expresses a different thought and feeling about liking or disliking the pie. This type of story should be presented 3–4 times. The practitioner should then try to get the child to participate in the story by pretending to taste a pie and giving his or her thoughts and feelings. If the child is successfully participating, then the practitioner should try to get the child to create a similar puppet story. The practitioner can practice this intervention several times implementing several different stories all with the same theme of each puppet having a different perspective. The practitioner can also discuss the concept of theory of mind with the child after each puppet story.

Rationale

This technique can work on any of the emotional regulation categories as they relate to learning theory of mind (when a child can understand that other people can have different thoughts and feelings from him or her about the same thing). The story can be about anything, as long as each puppet expresses a different thought and feeling. The puppet story should be animated and fun, and the practitioner should look for opportunities to get the child involved in the story and practicing taking different perspectives.

Theory of Mind (ToM) Puppets

My Emotions Cards

Primary Target Area	Emotional Regulation
Secondary Target Area	Social Skills
Level	Child and Adolescent
Materials	Blank Deck of Cards, Markers
Modality	Individual, Family, Group

Introduction

My Emotion Cards provides the opportunity for children and adolescents to create their own feelings card deck. The finished card deck can be used to play several games that help the child identify and share emotions. The practitioner can work with the child and the parents to establish several games that can be played with the card deck.

Instructions

The practitioner explains to the child that they are going to create their own card deck that focuses on feelings. Using a blank deck of cards (which can be purchased at most educational supply stores), the child is instructed to draw feeling faces on the cards and write the feeling word on the card as well. The child should make 2 of each feeling card so there is a matching card. The practitioner may have to help the child with writing and spelling and even identifying several feelings. The practitioner can also provide a feeling chart for the child to look at. The child should try to create as many feeling faces as he or she can think of and draw the faces as best as he or she can. It is also appropriate for the practitioner to make some cards and add them to the child's deck, especially if they are emotions that the practitioner knows that the child needs to work on. After the child has finished the card deck, the practitioner and child play some feeling card games together. Some examples would include Feelings Go Fish and Feelings Matching. The practitioner and child should try to think of other games that they could play with the feelings card deck, maybe even creating a new game.

Rationale

This technique can work on any of the emotional regulation categories depending on the variation of the games. The child can take the card deck home and play games with his or her parents. Several different games can be played, and the games can be played repeatedly. The child will likely not use all the blank cards, so he or she can take them home and add to the card deck as he or she discovers new feelings. The practitioner will likely have to share card game ideas with the parents and encourage them to think of new games to play.

6 Social Skills Interventions

Social Skills Cross-Off

Primary Target Area	Social Skills
Secondary Target Area	Behavior Change
Level	Child and Adolescent
Materials	Social Skills Cross-Off Sheet, Plastic Chip
Modality	Individual, Family, Group

Introduction

Children and adolescents with autism spectrum disorder often struggle in various areas of social skill development. Social Skills Cross-Off is an easily individualized intervention to help each child address his or her specific social skills deficits. The cross-off component of this intervention provides a fun and engaging way for children to practice social skills and stay on task until all the identified social skills have been addressed.

Instructions

The practitioner explains to the child that they are going to play a game and practice social skills. On a piece of white paper, the practitioner and child will create a 9 by 12 space grid (see example included here). The practitioner and child will work together to write different social skills in each of the 9 spaces. The practitioner will likely write most of the skills specific to what the child needs to work on, but the practitioner should ask the child for suggestions. The practitioner and child take turns flipping a plastic chip or a penny onto the grid. When a social skill is landed upon, the practitioner and child practice that skill. Once it has been practiced, the child crosses that skill off the grid. Practitioner and child keep playing until all skills have been practiced and crossed off the grid. When the grid is completed, the child earns a small prize or piece of candy.

Rationale

Social Skills Cross-Off helps children and adolescents develop a variety of social skills. The social skills that are written on the grid can be any social skills the child needs to work on and can be changed each time the game is played. The skills can also start out basic and become more complex as a child's social skills improve. Parents can be taught how to play the game and given ideas for social skills to write on the grid. Parents should try to play the game at home periodically and even involve other family members. The more the child can practice needed social skills the more likely he or she will be able to implement them in real situations.

Social Skills Cross-Off Worksheet

Show what you would do if a friend was trying to get you to do something wrong	Demonstrate some good manners
Make eye contact with someone while telling them something you did today	Introduce yourself and shake someone's hand
Show 3 emotions on your face without saying any words	Share a feeling and something that makes you feel that way
Make up a skit in which you are being polite to your teacher	Show what you would do if another child was making you mad
Practice listening to another person speak without interrupting them	Show 2 ways you could help your parents
Practice asking someone for help	Make up a skit in which you are being a good friend

Social Skills Pick-Up Sticks

Primary Target Area	Social Skills
Secondary Target Areas	Emotional Regulation, Connection, Behavior Change
Level	Child and Adolescent
Materials	Pick-Up Sticks Game, Social Skills Sheet
Modality	Individual, Family, Group

Introduction

This intervention provides an engaging game format to help children and adolescents practice and learn social skills. The common game of Pick-Up Sticks is used with an additional element designed to practice needed social skills. Practitioners are encouraged to create individualized social skill sheets for each child to address the skill deficits of the individual child they are working with.

Instructions

Using the game Pick-Up Sticks, the practitioner creates a sheet of paper with each pick-up stick color listed and several social skills to practice under each color (see example included here). The practitioner and child play a game of Pick-Up Sticks following the normal Pick-Up Sticks rules. When the child or practitioner picks up a stick of a certain color, they must look at the paper and pick one of the social skills listed under that color to practice. Skills should not be repeated, and play continues until all the sticks have been taken and all the skills practiced. It is important to note that some children will have trouble picking up some of the sticks without moving them. The practitioner should be lenient on this as the point is for the child to acquire a stick so he or she can practice a social skill.

Rationale

This intervention helps develop social skills, concentration and focus, fine motor skills, and even emotional regulation, depending on the skills chosen to address. Social Skills Pick-Up Sticks can be played several times, and the social skill sheet can be changed as needed to work on new or more complex skills. The practitioner should create the social skills list that matches the stick colors prior to the child beginning his or her session. Parents are taught the intervention, given a social skills sheet, encouraged to purchase a Pick-Up Sticks game, and asked to play at home with their child. Parents can create their own social skills sheets as needed.

Social Skills Pick-Up Sticks

Red

Make eye contact with someone for 10 seconds
Name 2 things that make a good friend
Name 3 fun things you could do with other people
Ask someone in the room a question
Give someone in the room a high five

Blue

Name something you could do that would cause you to lose a friend
Say some ways kids get bullied at school
Name 2 things you can do to feel less nervous
Talk about something you did with a friend
Act like you are playing your favorite sport

Yellow

Demonstrate the proper way to shake someone's hand
Introduce yourself and smile
Show an example of talking too loud, too soft, and just right
What are 2 positive things you could do if you get angry
Say 2 ways that you could help someone else

Green

Tell a story about something you did in less than 1 minute
Say something nice about someone else in the room
Ask someone in the room a question
Say 2 things that make you feel nervous
Talk about something fun you do at school

Black

Demonstrate a positive social skill
Show a positive social skill that you are good at

Magazine Minute

Primary Target Area	Social Skills
Secondary Target Areas	Emotional Regulation, Connection
Level	Child and Adolescent
Materials	Magazines
Modality	Individual

Introduction

Children and adolescents with ASD or other developmental disorders often struggle with a myriad of social situations. Many children with ASD experience high anxiety levels associated with social situations, and often these children try to avoid social situations. This intervention focuses on helping children identify social situations and talk about those situations to help increase skill and comfort level.

Instructions

The practitioner explains to the child that they will be using magazines to play a game that works on increasing social skills. The practitioner provides the child with several magazines. When the practitioner says, "go," the child will have 1 minute to go through the magazines to find and describe as many examples of someone doing something social as he or she can. The practitioner keeps track of how many examples the child presents in 1 minute. The practitioner also monitors the examples to make sure they are accurate. After the minute has passed, if there were some inaccurate examples, the practitioner discusses them with the child. The child can have several turns to see if he or she can increase his or her number each turn. The practitioner and child can switch roles with the child timing the practitioner and the practitioner finding the social examples. Switching turns provides the practitioner with the opportunity to model and talk about various social situations, especially ones that the child may be struggling with. This technique should be played multiple times for practice and mastery.

Rationale

Magazine Minute works on developing social skills, especially helping children to identify and talk about social situations. If the child is struggling with finding examples and seems unsure, this intervention may be too advanced for him or her. A variation of the intervention is used to work on emotional regulation. Instead of finding social situations and explaining them, the child has to find examples of someone showing an emotion and explain what is happening. Parents are taught this game and encouraged to implement the intervention at home.

Magazine Minute

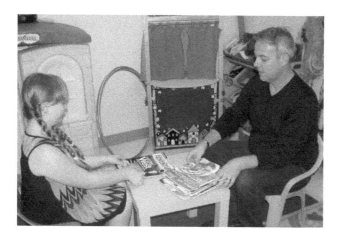

Action Identification

Primary Target Area	Social Skills
Secondary Target Area	Behavior Change
Level	Child and Adolescent
Materials	None
Modality	Individual

Introduction

Children and adolescents with ASD often struggle with appropriate behaviors in various situations. Action Identification is a fun and interactive game that helps children recognize appropriate versus inappropriate behavior to do in certain situations and provides the opportunity to practice appropriate responses.

Instructions

The practitioner writes various behaviors/actions on index cards (see example included here). The practitioner acts out an action such as running, talking, reading a book, playing a video game, eating, etc. The child has to guess what the action is and say in what situations it would be appropriate to do that action and in what situations it would be inappropriate to do the action. The practitioner can go through several different behaviors/actions, and if the child cannot identify the appropriate versus the inappropriate places and situations to do the behavior, the practitioner should help the child. The practitioner and the child can also switch roles, and the child can act out an action; the practitioner has to guess it and say when it would be appropriate and when it would not be appropriate. Some more example actions include yelling, picking your nose, bouncing a ball, sleeping, taking your shirt off, and playing with friends.

Rationale

Action Identification helps develop social skills, specifically helping children identify when certain behaviors are appropriate to do and in what context or situations behaviors would be inappropriate. The actions that the practitioner selects should be actions that the child currently has difficulty with in terms of doing them at inappropriate times. If the practitioner is unsure, then asking the parents for suggestions would be appropriate. Parents are taught this technique and are instructed to play the technique at home each day focusing on a few specific actions/situations that the child is having difficulty with.

Action Identification Cards

Running	Talking	Playing a Video Game	Eating
Reading a Book	Yelling	Picking Your Nose	Bouncing a Ball
Sleeping	Taking Your Shirt Off	Playing with Friends	Listening to Music
Hitting	Telling a Joke	Hugging Someone	Saying "No"
Playing with Your Parents	Playing Outside	Cleaning Up	Watching TV

Social Skills Bag

Primary Target Area	Social Skills
Secondary Target Areas	Connection, Behavior Change
Level	Child
Materials	Paper Bag, Art Decorations, Markers, Paper, Scissors
Modality	Individual, Group

Introduction

This intervention provides a child with repetitive practice of skills that he or she needs to gain. The social skills can be related to making friends or generalized to any social skill the child needs to improve.

Instructions

The practitioner explains to the child that they will be using a paper bag to make a social skills bag. The practitioner gives the child a small paper bag and instructs him or her to decorate it anyway that he or she likes and try to include things on the bag that describe him or her. Once the bag has been decorated, the practitioner and child work together to write, on 7 strips of paper (one for each day of the week), different social skills that the child needs to work on improving. After the skills have been written, the strips are put into the bag. If there is time remaining in the session, the practitioner and child can practice the social skills. The child is instructed to take the bag home, and each day, he or she will draw out one of the strips of paper and practice that skill 3 different times that day (with parents). In the next counseling session, child, parents, and practitioner review how the practicing went at home. The social skills practiced will most likely be chosen by the practitioner, but the child should be included, and he or she can write down any social skills that he or she believes need improvement.

Rationale

This technique is designed to work on a variety of social skills. Parents should be taught how the Social Skills Bag works and instructed to practice each day a social skill chosen from the bag. It is important that the parent and child practice the same skill 3 times each day. The more practice, the better the skill development. If a child needs more practice with the skills, then the same bag can be practiced for another week or more. New Social Skills Bags can also be created at any time to work on more social skills. A variation of this technique is an Emotion Bag, which would focus on one emotion such as worry, and the strips of paper would each have instructions on how to process and express worry. The same process would be followed with the child drawing one strip of paper out of the bag each day and practicing the idea for how to express his or her feelings of worry.

Social Skills Bag

Friendship Universe

Primary Target Area	Social Skills
Secondary Target Area	Connection
Level	Adolescent
Materials	Paper, Markers, Pencil
Modality	Individual, Group

Introduction

Adolescents with ASD often struggle with accurately identifying what constitutes a friend. Some adolescents with ASD will label a child at school that they have spoken to once as a good friend. Friendship Universe helps adolescents learn about and understand different levels of relationship in the sense of how well a person is known and different levels of friendships. It provides the opportunity for practitioner and adolescent to discuss current friendships in the adolescent's life and serves as both an assessment and social skill development intervention.

Instructions

The practitioner explains to the adolescent that they will be doing an activity that identifies the adolescent's current friendships. The practitioner and adolescent draw planets on a piece of paper (see example included here). The adolescent writes his or her name in the largest circle of the planet system. Each planet in the system will represent different friends in the adolescent's life. The adolescent will write the names of the friends who are closest (emotionally) to him or her in the planets closest to the adolescent. The friends who are not as close to the adolescent will have their names written in the planets that are farther away from the adolescent's name. Friends can include family members. Once the adolescent has finished, the practitioner and adolescent will talk about what the adolescent has created and the different levels of friendships, close friends versus acquaintances. The practitioner will likely have to spend time discussing how well the adolescent knows some of the people he or she has written down and conceptualizing what constitutes a close friend.

Rationale

This technique focuses on developing social skills related to friendships and relationships. This technique can be shared with parents so they can further talk with their child about friendships and help reinforce the concepts. It is not a technique that needs to be practiced at home throughout the week. It can be revisited in sessions with the practitioner. The practitioner may have the adolescent create a new friendship universe periodically to see if there are changes.

Friendship Universe

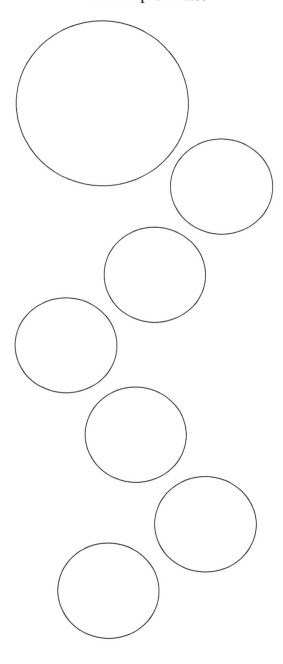

Role-Play

Primary Target Area	Social Skills
Secondary Target Area	Behavior Change
Level	Child and Adolescent
Materials	None
Modality	Individual, Family, Group

Introduction

Children and adolescents with ASD and other developmental disorders benefit greatly from role-playing through situations. Practitioners have the ability to identify several situations where a child or adolescent may need to improve their social functioning or their behaviors. Role-playing should be about the child and his or her situation and about real situations the child struggles with. Role-plays can be fun and engaging and include props and other people.

Instructions

The practitioner explains to the child that they are going to role-play some situations the child has been struggling with. The practitioner and child will decide on various social situations to role-play and social skills to work on during the role-plays. Some typical examples include recognizing when someone does something on purpose or accident, how to act when winning and losing, when to talk and when to listen, how to ask a teacher a question, saying hello and goodbye, how to respond to a bully, etc. Role-plays should be practiced several times throughout a session. Repetition and practice are essential for skill acquisition. The more the child can role-play situations and behaviors, the more likely he or she will be able to implement the desired behaviors during a real situation.

Rationale

This technique helps develop social skills through a role-play. The practitioner and child can work on a whole variety of social skills. One of the best ways to work on social skill development for children with ASD is through role-play. The practitioner can pick any scenario; role-play through it with the child; and cover how to act, respond, or handle the situation. When doing a role-play, it is best to avoid working in metaphors or in an approximation to the child's situation; instead, focus should be on directly talking about the child and what he or she should do in a situation. Role-plays can be taught to parents, and parents can practice the role-plays at home with their child. Parents can also role-play any situation that comes up that they feel needs attention. Some more common examples that a child with ASD might need to practice include how to act in a restaurant, using your manners, how to act in the car, what to do when your sibling makes you mad, doing chores, etc.

Common Role-Play Scenarios

How to respond when winning and losing

When to talk and when to listen

How to ask a teacher a question

Saying "hello" and "goodbye"

How to behave in a restaurant

How to order your own food in a restaurant

Saying "please" and "thank you"

How to behave in the car

What to do when your sibling makes you mad

How to behave when your parents ask you to do some chores

How to behave when standing in line and waiting for something

Different tones of voice for different situations

How to behave when you are getting your hair cut

How to behave when you are in the doctor's office

Making eye contact when talking to someone

How to behave at the dinner table

How to take care of a pet

How to play with other children

Giving someone else a compliment

How to handle peer pressure

Understanding appropriateness with humor

Candy Kindness Activity

Primary Target Area	Social Skills
Secondary Target Areas	Connection, Behavior Change
Level	Child
Materials	Paper, Aluminum Foil, Markers, Art Decorations, Glue
Modality	Individual, Family, Group

Introduction

This intervention offers a fun and expressive way for children to recognize how to be kind to others and practice acts of kindness. Often children with ASD have a difficult time showing positive expression to others. This intervention helps children recognize what a kind action toward another person would look like and gives the child the opportunity to implement kind actions.

Instructions

The practitioner explains to the child that they are going to be making pretend candy and learning about ways to be kind to other people. The practitioner and child write on small pieces of paper various kinds of things the child could do for or to other people. The child then creates and decorates candy wrappers out of other pieces of paper or aluminum foil. The small pieces of paper with kind things written on them are placed inside the candy wrappers (one for each candy wrapper). The practitioner and child can make as many of the kindness candies as they want, but at least 7 should be made (one for each day of the week). The child takes the candies home and unwraps one each day and has to practice/do that kind thing that day. At the next session, the child will report back to the practitioner how the child did with implementing the kind actions. This intervention can be repeated several times with new kind actions being created or repeating previous ones. The practitioner will likely have to suggest ideas that the child could do but should ask for the child's input. If there is any remaining time left in the session, the practitioner and child can practice the kind actions.

Rationale

Candy Kindness Activity works on social skill development specifically noting other people and doing something kind for them. This technique is explained to the parents, and the parents are instructed to participate in unwrapping one candy per day and practicing the skill with their child. If the child needs to continue to work on the skills, he or she can practice for another week or more. Also, new candies can be created in sessions or at home to work on other social skill areas. The social skills placed in the candy wrappers do not necessarily have to be kind things; they can be any social skills that the child needs to develop.

Candy Kindness Activity

My Safety Wheel

Primary Target Area	Social Skills
Secondary Target Area	Behavior Change
Level	Child and Adolescent
Materials	Paper, Pencil
Modality	Individual, Group

Introduction

It is essential that children with autism spectrum disorder and other developmental disorders learn about safety. Many children with developmental issues are easily victimized in various ways and typically not sure how to handle themselves when they are in unsafe situations. Many children with developmental issues have a difficult time even recognizing unsafe situations. This intervention presents a visual representation of safe and unsafe people, things, and places that the child can take home and keep as a reminder.

Instructions

The practitioner explains to the child that they will be discussing safety issues. The practitioner and child divide a piece of paper into 8 quadrants (see example included here). The quadrants are labeled: "safe places," "safe people," "safe activities," "safe objects," "unsafe places," "unsafe people," "unsafe activities," and "unsafe objects." The child can decorate the quadrants if he or she would like. The practitioner asks the child to identify safe/unsafe things or people for each quadrant. The child writes the safe/unsafe things down in each appropriate quadrant. The practitioner talks to the child about the meaning of "safe" and "unsafe." The practitioner may need to help the child if he or she is not familiar with who and what is safe and unsafe. It is likely the practitioner will add things to each quadrant, but the child should write everything that he or she can think of first. The practitioner may have to spend time explaining the concepts of safe and unsafe, and the practitioner may have to do the writing if the child has poor writing skills or cannot write.

Rationale

This technique helps develop safety-related social skills and will likely look different for children versus adolescents in terms of content. The practitioner should make sure that safe/unsafe things and people are covered adequately. If the child leaves something out, then the practitioner should add it to the quadrant. The technique can be taught to parents, and parents can periodically reinforce the concept at home by going through the safety wheel with their child. Children will gain the most benefit from this intervention if they revisit it periodically and continue to practice learning what is safe and unsafe.

My Safety Wheel Worksheet

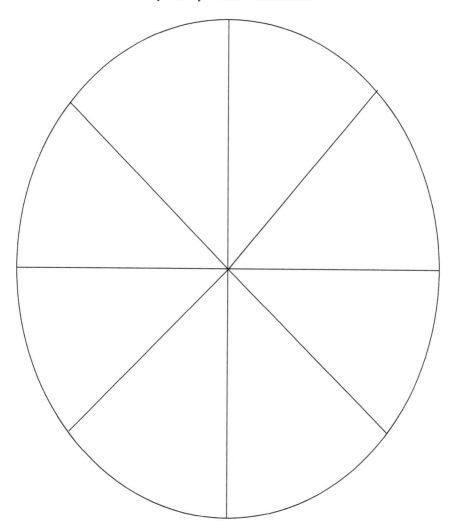

Conversation Bubbles

Primary Target Area	Social Skills
Secondary Target Areas	Behavior Change, Connection
Level	Child and Adolescent
Materials	Conversation Bubbles Worksheet, Pencil
Modality	Individual

Introduction

The Conversation Bubbles Worksheet helps children and adolescents practice what to say and how to say things in certain situations. It also provides the child with a written narrative to take home to help him or her remember what to say in certain conversations. This intervention works on general reciprocal conversation skills but can also be targeted toward specific types of conversations that the child may be struggling with.

Instructions

Using the Conversation Bubbles Worksheet (template included here), the practitioner begins by writing something in the first conversation bubble to begin the conversation. The child then has to write an appropriate response in the next bubble. The practitioner then writes a response to what the child wrote in the next bubble. This goes on until an appropriate end occurs. Once the conversation has ended, the practitioner should process through with the child how he or she felt being in the conversation and address any areas that could have been better. The practitioner and child can then begin a new conversation with the child going first. If the child is having difficulty coming up with a response, then the practitioner should help the child by giving him or her some appropriate examples. The conversation can be anything but is most helpful if the conversation is covering a real situation that the child is struggling with. The practitioner might begin with something like, "Hi, my name is Robert," or "Did you know school starts in two weeks?" or "Hi, can I help you find something in the library?"

Rationale

This technique works on developing social skills related to reciprocal conversation skills. It also works on fine motor skills and handwriting skills. The practitioner and child can complete as many Conversation Bubbles Worksheets as they want, covering many topics. Parents can also be trained in the technique and given a copy of the Conversation Bubbles Worksheet. Parents can periodically practice with their child at home especially covering any situation the child may have experienced where the conversation did not go well.

Conversation Bubbles Worksheet

What to Say? What to Do?

Primary Target Area	Social Skills
Secondary Target Areas	Behavior Change, Emotional Regulation
Level	Child and Adolescent
Materials	Index Cards, Pencil
Modality	Individual

Introduction

One of the primary issues that children and adolescents with ASD struggle with is being in and responding in social situations. This intervention provides the opportunity to discuss and practice a variety of social skills that a child or adolescent may need to improve. The practitioner can individualize this intervention and address specific situations that have been known to be challenging for the child.

Instructions

The practitioner explains to the child that they are going to work on how to respond in various social situations. The practitioner writes down several brief story scenarios on index cards. (This would likely be done before the child arrives for his or her session.) The practitioner reads one of the stories to the child. The child has to answer 1–2 questions about the story like "What would you say?" and "What would you do?" The stories should focus on scenarios that relate to the child's life. An example might be "One day a boy named Daniel [the client's name] was walking down the sidewalk. An older boy ran up to Daniel and told him he had to smoke a cigarette" (a real situation that happened that the client did not handle well). The child has to answer what he would do in this situation and/or what he would say. The practitioner will address any inappropriate responses or actions and help the child learn appropriate things to do and say. The practitioner and child should go through multiple stories discussing the child's responses. If the child is having a difficult time thinking of a response, then the practitioner should work with the child on learning appropriate responses.

Rationale

This intervention can work on a variety of social skills. The practitioner can address interactions, emotional responses, and connection elements with this intervention through the stories that the practitioner creates. The practitioner should write several stories before the session. After the technique has been done a few times, the practitioner can ask the child if he or she wants to create any stories. An additional element to this technique would be to role-play out the scenario after it is read with the child showing what he or she would say or do. Parents should be taught this technique to implement at home and practice periodically with their child.

Bubbles Social Skills

Primary Target Area	Social Skills
Secondary Target Area	Connection
Level	Child
Materials	Bubbles
Modality	Individual

Introduction

Children often need to practice skill deficits repeatedly in order to gain skills and be able to apply the skill in a real situation. This intervention uses bubbles to engage a child in practicing various social skills that are relevant for the child to improve. Several different social scripts or situations can be created using a bubble blowing process. This intervention is adapted from Liana Lowenstein's technique "Bubbles" found in *More Creative Interventions for Troubled Children & Youth*.

Instructions

The practitioner explains to the child that they are going to work on increasing social skills while blowing bubbles. The practitioner begins by creating a script to use with the bubbles. The practitioner reads the script to the child and tells the child that they are going to practice implementing the script using bubble blowing. Some examples include:

- **Introducing self, taking turns, and sharing:** The practitioner and child take turns blowing bubbles, one turn blowing the bubbles for each person. The practitioner starts by blowing the bubbles, the child then says, "Hi my name is _____, can I play with the bubbles?" The practitioner says, "Yes, I will share with you" and hands the child the bubbles. The child says "Thank you," and the practitioner says, "You are welcome." The child then blows the bubbles once, and the script is repeated back and forth. This will likely continue several times for practice and mastery.
- **Telling others you don't like something and hearing them tell you they don't like something:** The child blows the bubbles; the practitioner then says, "I don't like bubbles, please don't blow them by me." The child says "Sorry, I will blow them over here." Then the practitioner says, "Thank you."

Rationale

This technique helps develop various social skills. Parents can be taught Bubbles Social Skills to practice with their child. Parent and child are encouraged play Bubbles Social Skills at home practicing various skills. The practitioner will likely need to conceptualize several different scripts and teach the scripts to the parents, making sure the scripts are scenarios the child needs to work on.

Bubbles Social Skills

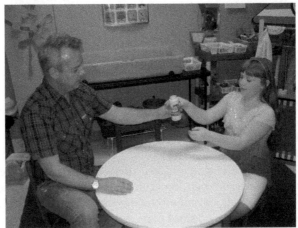

The Social Brick Road

Primary Target Area	Social Skills
Secondary Target Area	Behavior Change
Level	Child and Adolescents
Materials	Paper, Markers, Index Cards, Candy
Modality	Individual

Introduction

The Social Brick Road is a fun and creative way for a child or adolescent to work on improving any social skills where he or she has a deficit. The practitioner can design the intervention to address specific skills and repeat the game with new skills. Providing a small prize at the end of the intervention creates extra incentive for the child to participate.

Instructions

The practitioner and child create 5–7 pieces of paper drawn like bricks. The practitioner and child then discuss some social situations that do not go well for the child and write those on the back side of the brick paper. The practitioner and child then discuss an appropriate social skill, reaction, or response for each situation and write them on the back of the corresponding brick. The practitioner then places each paper brick on the floor around the playroom; the bricks should be placed in an order with a starting point and an ending point. The child is instructed to walk up to the starting brick, pick it up, and read the social problem and the suggestions for improvement. The practitioner and child will then role-play a scenario implementing the appropriate social skill. The child then moves on to the second brick and repeats the process until he or she gets to the final brick where a candy prize (or another type of prize) waits for him or her.

Rationale

This technique can help develop various social skills. The practitioner should choose social skills that the child needs to improve based upon real situations that the child currently experiences that do not go well. This intervention can be played through several times with new social skills bricks. Parents can be taught this technique and can be encouraged to play the game at home several times. The prize at the end of the road should be something that the child would enjoy earning such as a sticker, a piece of candy, or a small toy. When considering candy or any type of food as a prize, the practitioner should discuss this with the parents first to inquire about any allergies or special diets the child may have.

The Social Brick Road

Divide and Conquer

Primary Target Area	Social Skills
Secondary Target Area	Connection
Level	Child and Adolescent
Materials	Balloon
Modality	Individual, Family, Group

Introduction

Children and adolescents with ASD and other developmental disorders often have challenges in working with others and participating as part of a team. This intervention focuses on teaching children and adolescents how to notice others and work with other people to accomplish a task. It incorporates a teamwork concept in a fun and engaging game format.

Instructions

The practitioner explains to the child that they are going to play a game and that they have to focus on working together as a team. The practitioner and child each choose an area to stand in the playroom. The practitioner explains to the child that they can position themselves and their feet anywhere in the playroom, but once in place, they have to pretend that their feet are stuck to the floor and that they cannot move their feet. The practitioner and child hit a balloon in the air back and forth and try to keep it from touching the ground without moving their feet. The practitioner should spend some time discussing with the child the concept of working together and teamwork and that the only way to succeed at the game is by paying attention to each other and working as a team. The practitioner and child can also strategize and develop a plan to decide where each person will stand to cover the most playroom space. If the balloon hits the ground, the practitioner and child can decide on different places to stand and start over, seeing if they can keep the balloon in the air longer. This intervention also helps children understand personal space, self-control, and regulation.

Rationale

This technique helps develop social skills related to working as a team and working with another person to accomplish a task. It further promotes body awareness skills. The practitioner and child have to work together to keep the balloon from hitting the ground. The practitioner and child have to coordinate where they are going to stand to try and cover as much space as possible in the playroom and discuss how they are going to keep the balloon from touching the ground. This intervention can also be implemented in group format and can be taught to parents to play at home with their child and other family members can also participate.

Divide and Conquer

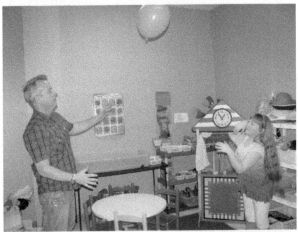

Pose

Primary Target Area	Social Skills
Secondary Target Areas	Emotional Regulation, Connection
Level	Child and Adolescent
Materials	Mirror
Modality	Individual

Introduction

Children and adolescents with ASD often have difficulty understanding their own bodies and the body language of others when they are in various social situations. This intervention focuses on teaching children and adolescents how to notice their affect, body language, and body responses. It also helps children understand how to recognize other people's body language.

Instructions

The practitioner explains to the child that they are going to be working on body language skills. The practitioner creates a list of various poses that the practitioner and child are going to perform. Each pose demonstrates a different type of body language or expression. The practitioner and child will each perform a pose from the list and perform it in front of a mirror so they can see themselves. As the child performs the pose, the practitioner will point out the different components of the child's body language, what the pose means or represents, and examples of when that type of body language would be appropriate or inappropriate. The practitioner can make the intervention more engaging by including props, such as wigs, hats, and dress-up clothes. The practitioner should go through several poses with the child, and this intervention can be repeated from session to session. Some example poses might be happy and sad poses, unfriendly and friendly poses, "leave me alone" poses, "I want to play" poses, tired poses, confused poses, proud poses, excited poses, normal poses, scared poses, feeling calm and out-of-control poses, etc.

Rationale

The Pose intervention helps children and adolescents work on improving social skills especially related to their body language. Many children with ASD will present as "flat" most of the time and will have a difficult time changing their body language and recognizing other people's body language. Parents can be taught this intervention to implement at home and can be encouraged to play with their child regularly and to note any gains when the child is able to display a variety of body language components in real situations.

Pose

7 Connection Interventions

Make My Moves

Primary Target Area	Connection (Relationship Development)
Secondary Target Areas	Sensory Processing, Social Skills, Anxiety Reduction
Level	Child
Materials	None
Modality	Individual, Family, Group

Introduction

Make My Moves is designed to help increase awareness of another person, increase connection with others, improve relaxation ability, and work on sensory-related issues (specifically vestibular and proprioceptive). This intervention is simple yet engaging and can incorporate many elements, can be played repeatedly, and can be taught to others easily.

Instructions

The practitioner explains to the child that they will be playing a game where they have to mimic each other's movements. The child and practitioner stand facing each other. One person is designated the leader. The leader makes various movements, such as moving arms up and down, moving legs, moving head back and forth, etc. The follower has to mimic the moves at the same time the leader is doing them (like a mirror effect). The practitioner should begin as the leader, and after a few minutes, the child can be the leader. The practitioner and child can switch back and forth with the leader role. The moves can vary in complexity and in speed (slow down and speed up). For decreasing anxiety and helping the child to relax, the practitioner should incorporate midline crossing moves—moves that activate the whole brain and crossing the right and left hemispheres. Several midline crossing moves can be found in the book *Brain Gym* by Paul and Gail Dennison.

Rationale

This technique is designed to work on connection and relationship development. It also works on social skills such as attuning to another person and making eye contact. It also functions as a brain-based play technique that helps children regulate and decrease their anxiety. The technique can be played repeatedly with each person switching roles as the leader. The practitioner will want to begin with slow and simple movements and progress as the child gets used to the technique. The practitioner should also try to incorporate moves that cross the midline and work on vestibular and proprioceptive sensory processing. This technique is taught to parents, and parents and children are encouraged practice the technique at home.

Make My Moves

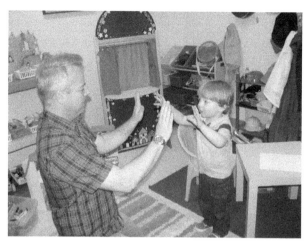

Follow My Eyes

Primary Target Area	Connection (Relationship Development)
Secondary Target Areas	Social Skills, Anxiety Reduction
Level	Child
Materials	None
Modality	Individual, Group

Introduction

Children with autism spectrum disorder often struggle with making and maintaining eye contact as well as focusing on another person. Often, trying to implement these skills will create a level of anxiety for the child. This intervention helps children address and work on developing these connection and social skills in a fun and engaging way that is less anxiety producing.

Instructions

The practitioner explains to the child that they will be playing a game and working on increasing eye contact with another person. The practitioner and child hold hands and stand facing each other. One person is designated the leader (the practitioner should be the leader first). The leader moves the two around the room using eye movements only to identify which direction they are going. No words are spoken and eye contact must be maintained the entire time and the practitioner and child must also keep holding hands. The practitioner should establish that looking to the right or left means moving in that direction and looking up means moving backward for the child and looking down means moving forward for the child. After about 5 minutes of play, the roles can be switched and the child can be the leader. The practitioner and child can play the game repeatedly switching back and forth in the leader role.

Rationale

This technique works on connection and relationship development. It also works on eye contact, attention, and focus skills as well as attuning to another person. The practitioner should start as the leader and begin with simple and slow movements. The speed and complexity can increase as the child gets used to the technique. The practitioner may need to remind the child to keep eye contact and continue to hold hands. Parents can be taught the intervention and instructed to play at home with their child. This intervention can also be implanted in a group format.

Follow My Eyes

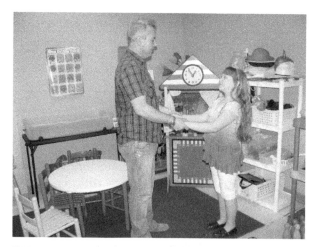

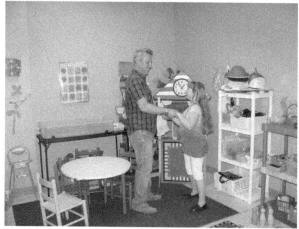

Body Bubbles

Primary Target Area	Connection (Relationship Development)
Secondary Target Areas	Social Skills, Anxiety Reduction
Level	Child
Materials	Bubbles
Modality	Individual

Introduction

Children with ASD often struggle to participate and play with another person. This intervention uses bubbles to engage with the child and gain the child's attention and focus in a playful game. It also works on helping the child gain connection skills. This intervention might be especially beneficial for children with lower functioning ability or children who do not do well attuning to another person or following directives.

Instructions

The practitioner explains to the child that they will be playing a game together using bubbles. The practitioner begins by blowing bubbles and instructs the child that he or she has to pop the bubbles before the bubbles hit the ground. After a few minutes of play, the practitioner tells the child that he or she has to pop all the bubbles before they hit the ground using a specific body part. For example, the practitioner might instruct the child that he or she has to pop the bubbles with his or her thumbs. After a few minutes of popping the bubbles this way, the practitioner might instruct the child that he or she has to pop the bubbles with his or her elbows. This continues for several rounds. Other body part examples include fingers, ears, nose, feet, shoulders, knees, and head. The practitioner and child can also switch roles with the practitioner popping the bubbles however the child decides.

Rationale

Body Bubbles helps to engage the child and create connection and relationship development skills. It also works on helping the child learn to attune to and play with another person. An added element to this technique would be to have the child say positive things about a family member while he or she is trying to pop all the bubbles. This intervention may start very basic with simply blowing the bubbles and having the child pop them; as the child is capable, more specific instructions can be added. This technique should be taught to parents. Parents should practice the intervention with their child at home. Other family members, such as an older sibling, can also be taught to play this game with the child at home.

Body Bubbles

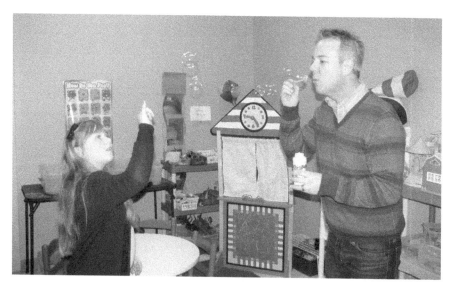

Family Name

Primary Target Area	Connection (Relationship Development)
Secondary Target Areas	Social Skills, Behavior Change
Level	Child and Adolescent
Materials	Paper, Markers, Art Decorations, Glue
Modality	Individual, Family

Introduction

Parents of a child with autism spectrum disorder often feel a loss of connection and meaningful relationship with their child. This intervention provides the opportunity for children to practice thinking about and expressing connection with their family members. Parents can also participate in this intervention, which provides a positive interaction between parent and child.

Instructions

The practitioner explains to the child that they will be creating an art project that describes the child's family. The practitioner and child draw the child's last name in bubble letters on a piece of paper. (For younger or more impaired children, the practitioner will likely draw the last name for the child.) The child's last name is then decorated by the child with things that remind the child of his or her family. The practitioner processes with the child what he or she has created and how it reminds him or her of his or her family. The child takes the finished name home and keeps it in his or her room or hangs it up somewhere in the home. Parents are taught how to implement this intervention and instructed to complete more Family Names at home with their child. The whole family can get involved, and each person can share and discuss their creations.

Discussion

Family Name works on connection and relationship development specifically with parents and other family members. It is designed to help the child think about his or her family and create something that shows the child's feelings of connection with his or her family. It also works on the social skill of thinking of and being aware of others. The child is creating something that is a concrete representation of a connection with his or her family, which can be positive for other family members to see. This activity should be repeated at home with the parents working with the child. All the decorated names should be displayed somewhere in the home.

Family Name

Construction Paper Decoration

Primary Target Area	Connection (Relationship Development)
Secondary Target Area	Sensory Processing
Level	Child and Adolescents
Materials	Construction Paper, String, Art Decorations, Scissors, Glue
Modality	Individual, Family, Group

Introduction

Children and adolescents with autism spectrum disorder often struggle with how to show or communicate care for another person. This intervention helps children focus on thinking about another person and doing something nice for that person. It also presents the opportunity to work on fine motor and sensory processing skills.

Instructions

The practitioner explains to the child that they will be creating things for each other out of construction paper. Construction paper, string, aluminum foil, or any other appropriate materials can be used in this intervention. The practitioner and child make items out of the materials to give to the other person. The items are decorative items the other person can wear, such as rings, hats, necklaces, bracelets, glasses, crowns, ties, belts, pins, etc. Once an object has been made, the person who made it physically places it on the other person. The practitioner and child can make several things for each other and completely decorate the other person. The intervention continues until the practitioner and child have finished making everything that they wanted to create for the other person. It is also beneficial to have a mirror present so the child can see him- or herself wearing the different items the practitioner has placed on him or her.

Rationale

This technique works on connection and relationship development, specifically thinking about another person, attuning to that person, and doing something nice for the other person. It is important that the process be reciprocal; the practitioner should make several items and place them on the child, and the child should make several items and place them on the practitioner. This technique is taught to parents, and parents should do the technique at home several times between sessions. Parents can also be encouraged to get other family members involved and participating with the child.

Construction Paper Decoration

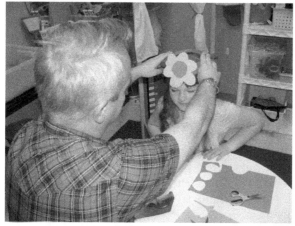

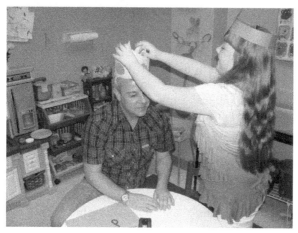

All around Me

Primary Target Area	Connection (Relationship Development)
Secondary Target Area	Social Skills
Level	Child and Adolescent
Materials	Miniatures
Modality	Individual

Introduction

All around Me is designed to help children think about and express positive sentiments about their family members. There is a symbolic component in this intervention where the child is asked to select miniatures to represent each person in his or her family. It is important to note that many children with ASD often struggle with symbolism. The practitioner should be aware of this and note that the child is capable of this level of symbolism before implementing this intervention.

Instructions

The practitioner explains to the child that they are going to play a game using miniatures. The child picks a miniature to represent each person in his or her family. The child sits on the floor and places the miniatures around him- or herself so the miniatures surround the child with each miniature facing the child. The child then turns and faces each miniature one at a time and tells the practitioner who the miniature represents and tells the practitioner something positive about that family member. The practitioner should also ask questions about each family member trying to get the child to expand on talking about each family member.

Rationale

This technique works on connection and relationship development specifically in regard to family relationships. It is important that the practitioner ask questions about each family member as the child is sharing about that particular family member. Many children will likely not share much information about the family member, so the practitioner questions are essential. This technique can be repeated several times in several different sessions with the practitioner. This technique is shared with parents but not expected to be done at home. Most parents will not have a miniature collection to be able to conduct this technique at home. One variation that parents could do at home is to have the child draw something to represent each person in his or her family and then share his or her drawing and discuss the family members.

All around Me

Soft Touches

Primary Target Area	Connection (Relationship Development)
Secondary Target Area	Sensory Processing
Level	Child
Materials	Several Soft Objects
Modality	Individual

Introduction

Children with ASD often have difficulties with physical touch. Soft Touches works on helping children become more comfortable with connection through physical touch. It also addresses sensory processing issues related to touch. Practitioners should fully explain this intervention to the child before beginning, especially to confirm that the child is comfortable with closing his or her eyes and experiencing touch/tactile sensation. The practitioner can demonstrate on him- or herself so the child understands what will be happening.

Instructions

The practitioner explains to the child that they will be playing a game using several different soft items and touching them to each other's skin. The practitioner instructs the child that the child is going to close his or her eyes and that the practitioner is going to touch some part of the child's skin with a soft object. (The child should be shown all the soft objects before the game begins.) The practitioner will then tell the child to open his or her eyes, and the child has to tell the practitioner which soft object touched him or her and where the soft object touched him or her on the skin. The practitioner will go through approximately 5–6 soft objects. Once the practitioner and child have gone through all the objects, they can switch roles. Some examples of soft objects include feathers, cotton balls, Kleenex, pieces of material, pipe cleaners, paint brushes, stuffed animals, pieces of ribbon, etc.

Rationale

This technique works on connection and relationship development especially in regard to becoming comfortable with touch sensation. This technique can be played repeatedly with new items being selected to use. After several rounds, the practitioner and child can switch roles. The practitioner should try to think of as many soft objects as he or she can to use in the game. The technique can be taught to parents and parents are instructed to play the technique at home with their child. Whether in session with the practitioner or at home with parents, it is important to be sensitive to the comfort level of the child with implementing this intervention.

Soft Touches

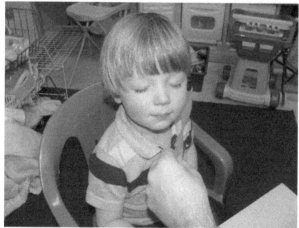

Candy Dandy

Primary Target Area	Connection (Relationship Development)
Secondary Target Areas	Social Skills, Anxiety Reduction
Level	Child
Materials	Candy
Modality	Individual, Group

Introduction

Children with autism spectrum disorder often struggle with awareness of their own body in relation to other people. Candy Dandy works on connection and sensory processing issues that help children become more aware of themselves, the space around them, and others. Candy is used as a reward to engage the child in participation. The practitioner should make sure the child can eat candy and is not on a special restriction or diet. If the child cannot eat candy, then many things can be substituted such as stickers or small toys as long as it is something the child enjoys.

Instructions

The practitioner explains to the child that they will be playing several games and that the child will have a chance to earn a candy reward. The practitioner should pick one of the child's favorite candies, such as M&Ms. (It is best to use a candy that has multiple pieces.) The practitioner will instruct the child to do various activities, and at the end of each activity, the child will get a piece of candy. Activities are short and focused on connecting with another person. Some example activities include spinning around in a circle, giving yourself a tight hug, doing some jumping jacks, flying around the room like an airplane, bending down and touching your toes, making your body into your favorite animal, holding hands and spinning around the room, playing patty cake, playing a game of tag, skipping around the room, rolling yourself into a ball, etc. Several example activities that can be incorporated into the intervention are included here.

Rationale

This technique works on connection, relationship development, body awareness, midline crossing, and vestibular and proprioceptive sensory processing. It is important to select a candy like M&Ms or Skittles, so one piece can be given after each activity. Some of the activities will go quickly. The practitioner can also repeat activities that he or she asks the child to perform especially if it is something the child enjoys. The technique is taught to parents to do at home, and parents are instructed to play the intervention periodically with their child.

Candy Dandy Example Activities

Shake hands

Give a hug

Make eye contact for 10 seconds

Give a double high five

Give a pat on the back

Play patty cake

Thumb wrestle

Paint finger nails

Brush hair

Throw a ball back and forth

Give a compliment to each other

Draw a picture together

Lotion each other's hands

Give a hand massage

Hit a balloon back and forth

Play the hand stack game

Blow bubbles

Sing a song together

Dance together

Ask each other a question

Make something for each other

Hats and Masks

Primary Target Area	Connection (Relationship Development)
Secondary Target Area	Social Skills
Level	Child
Materials	Various Hats and Masks
Modality	Individual

Introduction

Hats and Masks is a fun and inviting intervention for children with ASD and other developmental disorders. It includes a reciprocal element that helps children work on improving relationship and connection ability and improving paying attention to others. It also incorporates social skill development and improvement in joint attention skills.

Instructions

The practitioner explains to the child that they are going to play a game using several different hats and masks. This technique is usually done in a play therapy room but can be implemented in any setting as long as the practitioner provides several hats and masks and has access to a mirror. The practitioner presents several different hats and masks to choose from, and the practitioner and child take turns placing different hats and masks on each other and looking in a mirror to see how they look. The practitioner and child each choose the hat and mask they want the other person to wear and place that hat and mask on the other person. It is important that each person put the hat and mask on the other person, this process works on improving connection skills. It is also important to have a mirror close by so when the hats and masks are put on, the child can see him- or herself. The practitioner and child should play this intervention several times choosing several different hats and masks for each other. The technique can be expanded by seeing what other objects in the playroom can be turned into hats or masks.

Rationale

This technique works on connection and relationship development, especially in the area of attuning to another person and interacting with others. It is important that the game is reciprocal; the practitioner should place hats and masks on the child, and the child should place hats and masks on the practitioner. This provides opportunity for the child to pay attention and be aware of others. It also provides opportunity for eye contact and joint attention. The technique should be taught to parents, and parents are instructed to play the technique with their child at home several times throughout the week. If parents do not have a hat/mask collection, they can vary the intervention using other objects around the house that could be used as hats or masks.

Hats and Masks

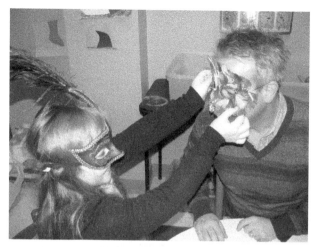

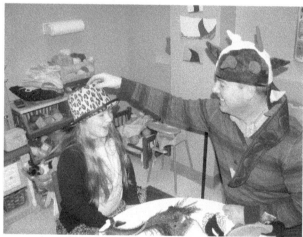

Tell Me about Your Family (Sand Tray)

Primary Target Area	Connection (Relationship Development)
Secondary Target Area	Social Skills
Level	Child and Adolescent
Materials	Sand Tray, Miniatures
Modality	Individual

Introduction

Children and adolescents with ASD often have a difficult time connecting with others even in their family relationships. Tell Me about Your Family Sand Tray works on increasing positive expression and connection with a child's family members. The practitioner should be aware of the symbolism involved in this intervention (miniatures are chosen by the child to represent members of his or her family) and the sensory element of the sand and make sure the child is comfortable with both before beginning.

Instructions

The practitioner explains to the child that they will be completing an activity using the sand tray. The practitioner should make sure the child is comfortable working in the sand. The practitioner instructs the child to select a miniature to represent each person in his or her family and place the miniatures in the sand tray. After the child is finished, the practitioner asks the child to say who each miniature is and tell something about that family member. The practitioner can also ask questions about the family members. The practitioner may have to help the child choose miniatures and help the child talk about his or her family members. If a child is having trouble selecting miniatures, then the practitioner could ask questions such as "What does your mom like to do?" or "Does your brother like computers?" Then, the practitioner could help the child select a miniature based on the child's answer. After the child has finished the sand tray and the sand tray has been discussed, the practitioner takes a picture of the sand tray, and the child takes the picture home and shares the picture of his or her sand tray with his or her family.

Rationale

This technique works on connection and relationship development especially related to family relationships. The technique can be done several times in several different sessions with the practitioner. It is unlikely that this technique will be taught to parents and implemented at home, as most parents will not have a sand tray collection of miniatures. The child can take a picture home and should share the picture with his or her family.

Tell Me about Your Family

Write and Move

Primary Target Area	Connection (Relationship Development)
Secondary Target Area	Sensory Processing
Level	Child and Adolescent
Materials	Paper, Markers
Modality	Individual

Introduction

Write and Move is an intervention that incorporates sensory processing with relationship development. This intervention is designed to work on physical connection between the child and another person as well as all 7 sensory processing areas: sight, smell, taste, hearing, touch, vestibular, and proprioceptive.

Instructions

The practitioner explains to the child that they will be creating and acting out a poem together. The poem will focus on the 7 sensory processing areas. The practitioner may begin by briefly explaining the 7 sensory processing areas. The practitioner and child work together to create a 7-line poem. Each line represents a different sensory experience. The practitioner and child write the poem and create movement to go with each line of the poem. The movements should connect child and practitioner physically. After the poem has been written and the movements have been decided, the practitioner and child say the poem and act out the movements together.

The poem follows the following script:

I see . . . I hear . . . I smell . . . I taste . . . I feel . . . I move . . . My body . . .

Rationale

This technique works on connection and relationship development by having the child work with the practitioner in creating the poem and movements. This technique also works on sensory processing regarding all 7 senses and can be taught to parents to do at home. Parent and child can create several different sensory poems at home. It is important that the movements that go with the poem are movements that physically connect the child with the practitioner or parent. This intervention involves a level of physical touch. The practitioner will want to make sure the child is comfortable with physical touch before implementing the intervention.

You, Me, and LEGO

Primary Target Area	Connection (Relationship Development)
Secondary Target Area	Social Skills
Level	Child and Adolescent
Materials	Several LEGOs
Modality	Individual, Group

Introduction

Many children and adolescents with ASD and other developmental disorders respond positively to playing with LEGOs. This intervention incorporates LEGOs and provides the opportunity for children to focus on their family members and practice working with another person to complete a task.

Instructions

The practitioner explains to the child that they will be completing an activity that involves working with LEGOs. The practitioner and child begin by each one building something out of LEGOs. The practitioner instructs the child that whatever he or she builds, it has to be something that would be in a family. The practitioner also builds something that would be in a family. Once the practitioner and child are finished, each one should share what he or she made that can be found in a family. The practitioner then instructs the child that they have to work together and combine what each one has created to make one object. The new combined object also has to be something that would be found in a family. More LEGOs can be added in the joining together phase, and after the practitioner and child are finished, each one can talk about what they made together and discuss the process of working together to create something.

Rationale

You, Me, and LEGO works on connection and social skills related to cooperation and working with others to complete a task. The practitioner should have a significant LEGO supply available to complete this technique, and the practitioner may want to limit the individual creation time to 10–15 minutes. It is important that the practitioner and child work together to combine their LEGO creations. The practitioner should not do all the work nor should the practitioner let the child do all the work; it should be a collaborative approach. The practitioner should spend some time talking to the child about what it feels like to work with someone else and have someone else share and implement his or her own ideas. The practitioner should ask the child about how times felt in his or her life when having to work with others to accomplish something.

You, Me, and LEGO

Family Bubbles

Primary Target Area	Connection (Relationship Development)
Secondary Target Area	Social Skills
Level	Child and Adolescent
Materials	None
Modality	Family, Group

Introduction

Children and adolescents and their family members often need to work on better relationship connection and especially participate in positive interactions. The Family Bubbles intervention works on increasing relationship development and some social skill development by having the family participate together in a playful and interactive game.

Instructions

The practitioner explains to the family that they will be playing a game together to work on connection. The practitioner explains that the family members are going to pair up and hold both hands with their partner. The practitioner is going to ask the family members to begin walking around the room while holding hands with their partner. The pair cannot touch any other family pair; if they do touch another family pair, then both pairs "pop," and they have to sit out until only one (or no) family pair remains. The practitioner should periodically change the instructions for the family pairs such as instructing them to hop around the room, skip around the room, walk in slow motion around the room, or move quickly around the room. This intervention works best when there are enough family members for at least 3 pairs. The practitioner can also participate if needed. If there is only a couple of family pairs, the practitioner can participate by moving around and trying to run into the pairs, and the pairs work together to try and avoid the practitioner.

Rationale

This intervention works on improving connection and relationship ability as well as social skill development related to working with another person and joint attention. It is designed as a family intervention but can also be used in groups, especially social skill groups. The practitioner will want to make the intervention fun and positive and focus on the experience, not make it a competition to see who can win. The intervention can be played repeatedly with the pairs switching to another family member so the child experiences being in a pair with each of his or her family members. Parents can implement this game at home with their family and play periodically between sessions.

Hula Hoop Exchange

Primary Target Area	Connection (Relationship Development)
Secondary Target Areas	Social Skills, Sensory Processing
Level	Child and Adolescent
Materials	2 Hula Hoops
Modality	Individual, Family, Group

Introduction

Children and adolescents with ASD and other developmental disorders often need to work on participating in a reciprocal way with others whether through an activity, a conversation, or in play. This intervention addresses increasing relationship with another person, working with another person in a reciprocal capacity, and sensory processing issues in the areas of vestibular and proprioceptive experience.

Instructions

The practitioner explains to the child that they will be playing several interactive games using hula hoops:

1. The practitioner and child stand about 4–5 feet from each other, facing each other. The practitioner and child each hold a hula hoop in their right hands. When the practitioner says, "Go," the practitioner and child will roll their hula hoops to the other person to catch. This goes back and forth several times.
2. The practitioner and child will each hold a hula hoop in their right hands, and when the practitioner says, "Go," the practitioner and child will each gently toss their hula hoop to the other person to catch. This goes back and forth several times.
3. Two hula hoops are placed on the floor beside each other. The practitioner and child each stand in one of the hula hoops. When the practitioner says, "Switch," the practitioner and child will jump into the other person's hula hoop. This goes back and forth several times.

The practitioner should demonstrate each hula hoop game before implementing with the child. Each hula hoop game can be played several minutes, and the child can be given an opportunity to think of other connecting hula hoop games.

Rationale

Hula Hoop Exchange works on increasing relationship connection, social skills, and vestibular and proprioceptive sensory processing. The practitioner should be aware of the child's physical abilities and adjust each hula hoop game accordingly. The practitioner will want to make sure that nothing is attempted at a level that could injure the child. This intervention can be taught to parents to play at home with their child. Hula Hoop Exchange can also be implemented in a group format.

Hula Hoop Exchange

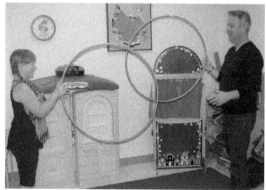

Let's Stick Together

Primary Target Area	Connection (Relationship Development)
Secondary Target Areas	Social Skills, Sensory Processing
Level	Child and Adolescent
Materials	None
Modality	Family, Group

Introduction

Many children and adolescents with ASD and other developmental issues need help in working on sensory processing issues, body awareness, interacting with other people as well as connection skills. Let's Stick Together is a fun and engaging intervention that incorporates movement to work on these skill areas. It is mainly designed to be implemented in a family setting but is also applicable to group work, especially social skills groups.

Instructions

The practitioner explains to the family that they will be playing a game together that works on increasing relationship connection. The practitioner explains that each person in the family will begin by moving around the room in a certain way, which the practitioner decides. After a few minutes, the practitioner will state a new way to move around the room. The movements can be things like walk around the room, skip around the room, hop around the room, walk backward around the room, etc. Each family member moves around the room as instructed and tries to avoid the other family members. If 2 people touch in any way, then they are now stuck together, and they continue moving around the room more tightly, pretending they are physically stuck to each other. Once 2 family members have gotten stuck together, they will actively try to catch other family members. Moving around the room in different ways continues until the whole family is stuck together. Once the whole family is stuck together, the practitioner can spend a few minutes having the whole family try to move around the room in different ways. The practitioner can also participate if more people are needed.

Rationale

This intervention helps children with ASD work on strengthening relationship connection especially with their family members. It also works on social skill improvement and sensory processing in the areas of vestibular, proprioceptive, and touch. This game can be played repeatedly with family members taking turns deciding what the movements will be. It is important to keep the intervention fun and noncompetitive. The practitioner should emphasize that the family focus on being playful and on enjoying the game together.

Let's Stick Together

Appendix
Additional Resources

Author's Note: This chapter contains various assessment materials, forms, and other useful worksheets that can be downloaded in a larger, printable format from www.autplaytherapy.com/resources.

Intake and Assessment Phase Guide

Session 1

1. Practitioner meets with parents only.
2. Complete and review intake forms. Give parents AutPlay inventories to compete and return in Session 2.
3. Collect background information and all relevant documents including any previous psychological evaluations, sensory evaluations, and IEP documents.
4. Explain the AutPlay process.

Session 2

1. Meet with parents and child. Collect AutPlay inventories from parents.
2. Take child on a tour of the facility, including playroom(s).
3. Focus on relationship development and helping the child become familiar and comfortable with the facility and the practitioner.
4. Conduct a child observation with the child in a playroom setting. Parents should observe via a monitor or from a corner of the playroom. Practitioners should utilize the AutPlay Child Observation form when conducting the observation. This observation should last approximately 30–35 minutes.

Session 3

1. Meet with parents and child. Address any questions or comments that parents or child may have.
2. Conduct a parent/child observation in a playroom setting. Practitioner should observe through monitor equipment or station him- or herself in one corner of the playroom. Practitioners should utilize the AutPlay Child/Parent Observation form when conducting the observation. This observation should last approximately 20–25 minutes.

3. Practitioners should use any remaining session time to meet with the child in the playroom and continue to work on relationship and rapport building.

Session 4

1. Meet with the parents and child. Spend the first half of the session meeting with the parents to discuss the observations and review the AutPlay inventories. Discuss treatment goals and decide on the logistics of how to conduct parent and child sessions moving into the directive intervention phase.
2. Use any remaining session time to meet with the child in a playroom and continue to develop relationship and rapport.

Parent Guide for Implementing the Follow Me Approach

1. Set the stage for your play times by choosing a day and time to have your play time and a location in your home for the play time. Be mindful to choose times and locations that will be the least distracting for you and your child. Avoid times and locations where you or your child may be distracted by other people, tasks, or objects in your surroundings.

2. Begin the play time with an introductory statement, such as "This is our special play time, you can play anything you want, and I will be in here with you."

3. Let your child lead the play time. He or she can choose to play with what he or she wants and how he or she wants. Follow your child as he or she transitions from one toy or activity to another. Try to stay physically close to your child.

4. Periodically make tracking and reflective statements.

5. Periodically ask your child questions.

6. Periodically try to engage with your child in what he or she is playing with. Look for opportunities to insert yourself into the play and notice instances where your child is accepting your attempts to engage and playing back with you.

7. Try to engage your child in ways that promote attunement and acknowledgment skills.

8. Be mindful of your child's limits. Do not push your child to engage with you to the point of dysregulating your child. If you feel that your child has reached his or her limit, then end the play time.

9. Make note of instances where your child demonstrates any of the basics skills that have been targeted and any advances in reciprocal play or interaction that your child produces.

10. End the play time with a closing statement, such as "In 5 minutes, our play time with be over." After 5 minutes, "Our play time is over; we will play again next time."

11. Write down any questions that arise and bring the questions with you to discuss with the practitioner during your next appointment.

Limit-Setting Guide in the Follow Me Approach

Children and adolescents with ASD may at times, engage in behaviors that require limit setting. Any behavior that could be harmful to the child or another person would require using the limit-setting protocol. Also, any behaviors that could result in a destruction of toys or property would require setting limits. Additionally, some practitioners and parents may have some standard guidelines such as no throwing sand out of the sand tray or no coloring on the walls, which would also require implementing the limit-sitting protocol.

Practitioners and parents should try to set limits as little as possible, but when a limit needs to be set, the following protocol is suggested:

First

1. Implement redirecting and/or replacement strategy. Redirecting involves moving the child and the child's attention to another more appropriate focus. Replacement involves providing the child a more acceptable way to do what he or she is currently doing that is not acceptable. Redirecting and replacement should be attempted several times to give the child opportunity to change his or her behavior before moving to removal.

   If behavior continues

Second

2. Verbally prompt child to discontinue behavior. It would be appropriate to give the child a couple of verbal prompts before removing the child. Also, verbal prompts should be given in a matter of fact way and spoken slowly and clearly to the child. Redirecting and replacement options can also be added to verbal prompts.

   If behavior continues

Final

3. Implement the removal process. This is a last option solution and should only be used if the practitioner or parent has sufficiently tried all other options and still feels the child or others are in a dangerous situation. Removal involves guiding the child out of the situation or space that he or she is currently in or removing objects from the child. In some cases with children with ASD, this might require forced physical removal of the child. If physical removal is required while working with the practitioner, parents should be the ones to implement the removal. When a child is removed, he or she should be taken to a location where there are no other people and relatively low-stimulation surroundings. The goal in removal is to help the child calm to keep him and others safe.

Feelings List

Accepted	Afraid	Affectionate	Loyal
Angry	Miserable	Anxious	Misunderstood
Peaceful	Beautiful	Playful	Ashamed
Brave	Awkward	Calm	Proud
Capable	Quiet	Bored	Overwhelmed
Caring	Relaxed	Confused	Cheerful
Relieved	Defeated	Comfortable	Safe
Competent	Satisfied	Concerned	Mad
Depressed	Pressured	Confident	Provoked
Content	Desperate	Regretful	Courageous
Silly	Lonely	Rejected	Curious
Special	Disappointed	Remorseful	Strong
Discouraged	Disgusted	Sad	Sympathetic
Excited	Embarrassed	Shy	Forgiving
Thankful	Sorry	Friendly	Thrilled
Fearful	Stubborn	Nervous	Stupid
Glad	Understood	Frustrated	Good
Unique	Furious	Tired	Grateful
Valuable	Guilty	Touchy	Great
Hateful	Happy	Helpless	Hopeful
Wonderful	Hopeless	Humorous	Worthwhile
Unattractive	Joyful	Uncertain	Lovable
Humiliated	Uncomfortable	Loved	Hurt
Ignored	Impatient	Indecisive	Inferior
Insecure	Irritated	Jealous	Worried

General Social Skills Checklist

NAME	DATE
☐ Listening	☐ Asking Questions
☐ Starting a Conversation	☐ Smiling
☐ Ending a Conversation	☐ Saying "Thank You"
☐ Introducing Self	☐ Making Eye Contact
☐ Introducing Other People	☐ Basic Boundaries
☐ Asking for Help	☐ Following Instructions
☐ Apologizing	☐ Asking Permission
☐ Sharing	☐ Joining in a Group
☐ Helping Others	☐ Taking Turns
☐ Appropriate Body Language	☐ Appropriate Tone of Voice
☐ Understanding Personal Space	☐ Two-Way Conversation
☐ Making and Maintaining Friends	☐ Public Boundaries
☐ Handling Losing	☐ Handling Winning
☐ Giving Instructions	☐ Convincing Others
☐ Negotiating	☐ Using Self-Control
☐ Handling Bullying	☐ Giving Compliments
☐ Accepting Consequences	☐ Managing Disagreements
☐ Recognizing Trouble Situations	☐ Understanding Humor
☐ Completing Tasks without Assistance	☐ Initiating Tasks
☐ Well-Rounded Play Skills	☐ Problem Solving
☐ Flexible	☐ Advanced Boundaries
☐ Expressing Emotions Appropriately	☐ Knowing Emotions
☐ Recognizing Emotions in Others	☐ Expressing Affection
☐ Expressing Concern for Others	☐ Handling Anxiety
☐ Emotion/Situation Appropriateness	☐ Showing Compassion
☐ Handling Anger-Related Feelings	☐ Avoiding Fights
☐ Dealing with Accusation	☐ Standing Up for Others
☐ Self-Relaxation Techniques	☐ Accepting "No"
☐ Other	

AutPlay Therapy Suggested Toys and Materials

TOYS	
Human miniatures/figures	Animal miniatures
Car, plane, and boat miniatures	Sand tray
Toy food, dishes, and kitchen area	Water tray
Set of building blocks	Set of LEGOs
An assortment of various balls	Sensory balls and toys
Hula hoops	Rope
An assortment of hats and masks	Mirror
Balloons	Bubbles
Toy phone	Toy computer
Basketball	Basketball goal
Doctor's kit	Cash register
Large cardboard bricks	Toy money
Toy musical instruments	Nerf guns
Foam swords (pool noodles)	Beach ball
Mr. Potato Head game	Feeling face cards
iPad	CD Player
EXPRESSIVE MATERIALS	
White paper	Construction paper
Paints/markers/crayons	Blank puzzles
An assortment of art (decoration) supplies	Stickers
Clay/Play Doh	Magazines
Dry erase board	Dry erase markers
An assortment of art (construction) supplies	Buddha Board

AutPlay Child Observation Form

Child's Name_____Age___Gender___Date_____

Verbal Ability (Does the child make any verbal comments? Are comments relevant/ understandable? Does the child engage in conversation and answer questions?)

_____

_____

_____

Play Skills (What does the child play with? Does the child play with any toys? Does the child play with toys appropriately in regard to toy function and child's age? How much time is spent on toys played with?)

_____

_____

_____

Social Interactions (Does the child respond in an appropriate social manner? Does the child use age appropriate social skills in interacting with practitioner? What social skills are observed and what social skills seem lacking?)

_____

_____

_____

Attention/Focus/Impulsivity (Does the child maintain attention for appropriate amount of time? Does the child wander around the room continuously? Does the child keep focus on toys, complete tasks, and does the child appear impulsive?)

_____

_____

_____

Withdrawn/Isolating Behaviors (Does the child interact with practitioner? Does the child seem to withdraw into own world? Does the child seem to notice or respond to practitioner being in the room? Does the child attempt to connect with practitioner?)

_____

_____

_____

AutPlay Child/Parent Observation Form

Child's Name_____Age___Gender___Date_____

General Child and Parent Interactions (Describe the overall interaction between parent and child. Do interactions occur smoothly? Does the child seem to listen to, respond to, and engage parent?)

_____

_____

_____

Joint Play, Child and Parent Together (Do child and parent play together? Describe type, quality, and quantity of play together. Is play together forced or natural?)

_____

_____

_____

Verbal and Nonverbal Reciprocal Communication (Do child and parent engage in verbal reciprocal communication? Does the child respond to parent with verbal communication? Do child and parent exchange nonverbal communication? Does the child notice parent's nonverbal communication?)

_____

_____

_____

Parent Initiations Toward Child (Does parent initiate interaction with child? How does parent attempt to initiate with child? How does the child respond to parent initiations?)

_____

_____

_____

Joint Attention Interactions (Do child and parent engage in joint attention? If so, how often, and does joint attention occur naturally?)

_____

_____

_____

AutPlay Autism Checklist

Child's Name_____Age___Gender____Date_____

The AutPlay Autism Checklist is an autism screening instrument to help assess the need for further evaluation. Place a check by each statement that describes your child. If you are unsure, leave the statement blank. A score of 3 or more checks may indicate the need for further evaluation.

___Makes little or no eye contact

___Lacks eye-to-eye gaze

___Little or no facial expression

___Lacks gestures and nonverbal behaviors that regulate social interaction

___Failure to develop peer relationships appropriate to developmental level

___A lack of spontaneous seeking to share enjoyment, interests, or achievements with other people

___Lack of social or emotional reciprocity (not actively participating in simple social play or games)

___Prefers solitary activities or involving others in activities only as tools or "mechanical" aids

___Impairments in verbal communication

___Delay in or total lack of the development of spoken language

___If adequate speech, marked impairment in the ability to initiate or sustain a conversation with others

___Stereotyped and repetitive use of language or idiosyncratic language

___Lack of varied, spontaneous make-believe play or social imitative play appropriate to developmental level

___Restricted repetitive and stereotyped patterns of behavior, interests, and activities

___Preoccupation with one or more stereotyped and restricted patterns of interest that is abnormal either in intensity or focus

___Inflexible adherence to specific, nonfunctional routines or rituals

___Stereotyped and repetitive motor mannerisms (e.g., hand or finger flapping or twisting)

___Persistent preoccupation with parts of objects

___Early childhood delays or abnormal functioning in social interaction

___Early childhood delays or abnormal functioning in language as used in social communication

___Early childhood delays or abnormal functioning in symbolic or imaginative play

About the AutPlay Autism Checklist

The checklist is based upon the DSM-V diagnostic criteria for autism spectrum disorder. It is valid for children ages 3–18. The checklist is designed to be completed by a parent or other caregiver who is around or involved enough with the child or adolescent to provide accurate feedback. Practitioners should use the checklist in the following ways:

1. As part of an autism screening procedure to determine if further evaluation is needed to detect autism spectrum disorder.
2. As an assessment tool to gain further information about a child or adolescent's skill strengths and deficits.
3. As an assistance in developing treatment goals.

Instructions for Completing the AutPlay Autism Checklist

Practitioners should give the checklist to parents or other caregivers who would be knowledgeable about the child. (This might include foster parents, schoolteachers, nannies, or other relatives.) Parents are instructed to complete the checklist by placing a check next to any statement that they feel describes their child. Parents are **not** given a copy of the "About the AutPlay Autism Checklist" sheet. Practitioners should review the results and proceed accordingly.

Scoring

Three or more checks may indicate the need for further evaluation. When completing the AutPlay Autism Checklist as part of an autism screening, practitioners should compare results on the checklist with other screening inventories or procedures as part of a comprehensive screening and look for additional signs that further evaluation is warranted. The checklist should not be used in isolation to address an autism screening.

Practitioners looking for more resources for conducting autism screenings should consider conducting a child observation, a parent/child observation, and implementing additional inventories such as the Autism Treatment Evaluation Checklist and the Modified Checklist for Autism in Toddlers (M-CHAT). Practitioners should refer parents for a full evaluation if there is any indication that Autism Spectrum Disorder may exist.

AutPlay Emotional Regulation Inventory: Child (3–11)

Child's Name_____Age____Gender____Date_____

Rate the following emotional regulation abilities on the continuum from not developed to developed with a "1" being not developed at all and a "5" being sufficiently developed. Try to recall situations with your child and adequately assess his or her level of proficiency. If you are unsure, leave blank.

My child verbalizes positive emotions.

1   2   3   4   5

My child verbalizes negative emotions.

1   2   3   4   5

My child shows appropriate body language to match an emotion.

1   2   3   4   5

My child can differentiate between at least 5 emotions.

1   2   3   4   5

My child recognizes when another person is feeling something.

1   2   3   4   5

My child can accurately identify an emotion in another person.

1   2   3   4   5

My child understands anxiety and can self-calm.

1   2   3   4   5

My child understands anger and knows anger-reducing strategies.

1   2   3   4   5

My child can verbalize when he or she feels angry or anxious.

1   2   3   4   5

My child shows emotions in pretend or symbolic play.

1   2   3   4   5

My child can verbalize when he or she feels confused.

1   2   3   4   5

My child can identify an emotion that goes with a certain situation such as what someone would feel when they are at a funeral.

1   2   3   4   5

AutPlay Emotional Regulation Inventory: Child (3–11)

Please answer the following questions regarding your child's emotional regulation. Try to think about specific times you have observed your child and answer the questions as completely as possible.

1. Describe a situation in which your child appropriately expressed an emotion.

2. Describe a situation where your child was expressing a negative emotion and was able to self-calm.

3. Describe a situation when your child accurately identified an emotion in another person.

4. Describe how emotions are shown and expressed in your family.

5. Describe how emotions are currently taught and or modeled for your child.

AutPlay Emotional Regulation Inventory: Adolescent (12–18)

Child's Name_____Age____Gender____Date_____

Rate the following emotional regulation abilities on the continuum from not developed to developed with a "1" being not developed at all and a "5" being sufficiently developed. Try to recall situations with your child and adequately assess his or her level of proficiency. If you are unsure, leave blank.

My child verbalizes positive emotions.

1   2   3   4   5

My child verbalizes negative emotions.

1   2   3   4   5

My child shows appropriate body language to match an emotion.

1   2   3   4   5

My child can differentiate between at least 10 emotions.

1   2   3   4   5

My child recognizes emotions in others.

1   2   3   4   5

My child can accurately identify an emotion in another person.

1   2   3   4   5

My child understands anxiety and can self-calm when anxious.

1   2   3   4   5

My child understands anger and knows anger-reducing techniques.

1   2   3   4   5

My child can verbalize when he or she feels angry or anxious.

1   2   3   4   5

My child shows emotion in regard to peer and family relationships.

1   2   3   4   5

My child seems to understand and express empathy.

1   2   3   4   5

My child can identify an emotion that goes with a certain situation such as what someone would feel when they are at a funeral.

1   2   3   4   5

AutPlay Emotional Regulation Inventory: Adolescent (12–18)

Please answer the following questions regarding your child's emotional regulation. Try to think about specific times you have observed your child and answer the questions as completely as possible.

1. Describe a situation in which your child appropriately expressed an emotion.

2. Describe a situation where your child was expressing a negative emotion and was able to self-calm.

3. Describe a situation when your child accurately identified an emotion in another person.

4. Describe how emotions are shown and expressed in your family.

5. Describe how emotions are currently taught and or modeled for your child.

AutPlay Social Skills Inventory: Child (3–11)

Name _____Age____Gender ____Date _____

Rate the following social skills on the continuum from not developed to developed with a "1" being not developed at all and a "5" being sufficiently developed.

SKILL	Not Developed			Developed	
Says "hello" to others	1	2	3	4	5
Makes eye contact with others	1	2	3	4	5
Plays with other children	1	2	3	4	5
Shows kindness to others	1	2	3	4	5
Shares with others	1	2	3	4	5
Listens without interrupting	1	2	3	4	5
Asks questions	1	2	3	4	5
Answers questions when asked	1	2	3	4	5
Talks about feelings	1	2	3	4	5
Shows appropriate body language	1	2	3	4	5
Understands other people's body language	1	2	3	4	5
Asks for help	1	2	3	4	5
Follows rules	1	2	3	4	5
Includes other children in his or her play	1	2	3	4	5
Understands other's point of view	1	2	3	4	5
Handles anger/frustration	1	2	3	4	5
Asks to play with other children	1	2	3	4	5
Understands teasing and bullying	1	2	3	4	5
Ignores teasing and bullying	1	2	3	4	5
Speaks in appropriate tone of voice	1	2	3	4	5
Speaks at appropriate rate	1	2	3	4	5
Speaks clearly	1	2	3	4	5
Feels sorry for inappropriate behaviors	1	2	3	4	5
Responds when spoken to	1	2	3	4	5
Understands social boundaries	1	2	3	4	5
Knows safety information	1	2	3	4	5
Has friends his or her own age	1	2	3	4	5
Knows how to make friends	1	2	3	4	5

Asks other children to play with him or her	1	2	3	4	5
Accepts response of "no"	1	2	3	4	5
Ignores distractions	1	2	3	4	5
Understands appropriate behaviors in public	1	2	3	4	5
Expresses a desire to play with peers	1	2	3	4	5
Talks appropriately (not too much or too little)	1	2	3	4	5
Understands manners	1	2	3	4	5
Participates appropriately in peer groups	1	2	3	4	5
Talks to adults	1	2	3	4	5
Acknowledges other people's presence	1	2	3	4	5
Solves problems	1	2	3	4	5
Verbally expresses feelings	1	2	3	4	5

AutPlay Social Skills Inventory: Adolescent (12–18)

Name _____Age____Gender ____Date _____

Rate the following social skills on the continuum from not developed to developed with a "1" being not developed at all and a "5" being sufficiently developed.

SKILL	Not Developed			Developed	
Introduces self to others	1	2	3	4	5
Makes eye contact with others	1	2	3	4	5
Socializes with other children his or her age	1	2	3	4	5
Shows empathy to others	1	2	3	4	5
Shares with others	1	2	3	4	5
Listens without interrupting	1	2	3	4	5
Identifies needs in others and will help	1	2	3	4	5
Asks for help	1	2	3	4	5
Talks about feelings	1	2	3	4	5
Displays appropriate body language	1	2	3	4	5
Understands other's body language	1	2	3	4	5
Ends a conversation	1	2	3	4	5
Enters a conversation	1	2	3	4	5
Includes others in what he or she is doing	1	2	3	4	5
Understands other's point of view	1	2	3	4	5
Handles anger/frustration appropriately	1	2	3	4	5
Knows how to join a group	1	2	3	4	5
Follows rules	1	2	3	4	5
Knows how to compromise	1	2	3	4	5
Speaks in appropriate tone of voice	1	2	3	4	5
Speaks at appropriate rate	1	2	3	4	5
Accepts response of "no"	1	2	3	4	5
Accepts responsibility for actions	1	2	3	4	5
Responds when spoken to	1	2	3	4	5
Knows appropriate social boundaries	1	2	3	4	5
Knows safety information	1	2	3	4	5
Expresses own opinions	1	2	3	4	5
Makes friends with others	1	2	3	4	5

	1	2	3	4	5
Can initiate tasks on own	1	2	3	4	5
Expresses concern for others	1	2	3	4	5
Ignores distractions	1	2	3	4	5
Can give directions	1	2	3	4	5
Can explain things to others	1	2	3	4	5
Apologizes for mistakes	1	2	3	4	5
Understands manners	1	2	3	4	5
Cooperates and participates in peer groups	1	2	3	4	5
Talks to adults	1	2	3	4	5
Understands teasing and bullying	1	2	3	4	5
Solves problems	1	2	3	4	5
Uses appropriate hygiene	1	2	3	4	5

AutPlay Connection Inventory: Child (3–11)

Child's Name_____Age_____Gender_____Date_____

Rate the following connection-related skills on the continuum from not developed to developed with a "1" being not developed at all and a "5" being sufficiently developed. Try to recall situations with your child and adequately assess his or her level of proficiency. If you are unsure, leave blank.

My child gives hugs and other appropriate engaging physical touch.

1   2   3   4   5

My child says, "I love you" and/or makes other endearing verbal statements.

1   2   3   4   5

My child receives hugs and other engaging physical touch.

1   2   3   4   5

My child cries and/or appears sad when something occurs that would warrant this emotional response.

1   2   3   4   5

My child displays empathy toward others.

1   2   3   4   5

My child makes appropriate eye contact.

1   2   3   4   5

My child is inconsistent in his or her affection toward family members.

1   2   3   4   5

My child appears unable to give or receive love.

1   2   3   4   5

My child appears to avoid physical closeness and touch.

1   2   3   4   5

My child initiates games and play with others.

1   2   3   4   5

My child will participate if games or play are initiated by others.

1   2   3   4   5

My child responds appropriately when others engage him or her.

1   2   3   4   5

My child talks about or seems interested in being with other family members or peers.

1   2   3   4   5

AutPlay Connection Inventory: Adolescent (12–18)

Child's Name_____Age_____Gender_____Date_____

Rate the following connection-related skills on the continuum from not developed to developed with a "1" being not developed at all and a "5" being sufficiently developed. Try to recall situations with your child and adequately assess his or her level of proficiency. If you are unsure, leave blank.

My child gives hugs and other appropriate engaging physical touch.

1   2   3   4   5

My child says, "I love you" and/or makes other endearing verbal statements.

1   2   3   4   5

My child receives hugs and other engaging physical touch.

1   2   3   4   5

My child will cry or display other appropriate sad emotions if the situation warrants such a response.

1   2   3   4   5

My child displays empathy toward others.

1   2   3   4   5

My child makes appropriate eye contact.

1   2   3   4   5

My child is inconsistent in his or her affection toward family members.

1   2   3   4   5

My child appears unable to give or receive love.

1   2   3   4   5

My child appears to avoid physical closeness and touch.

1   2   3   4   5

My child initiates games or "hang out" time with peers.

1   2   3   4   5

My child will participate if other peers initiate games or "hang out" time.

1   2   3   4   5

My child participates in or seems to want to participate in peer activities.

1   2   3   4   5

My child seems to have an appropriate parent/adolescent relationship connection.

1   2   3   4   5

AutPlay Assessment of Play Skills

Child's Name_____Age____Gender____Date_____

Read the following play categories and definitions and rate where you feel
your child is at in terms of possessing and demonstrating this type of play.

Functional play is a term also used for relational play. It denotes the use
of objects in play for the purposes for which they were intended, e.g.,
using simple objects correctly, combining related objects (a female doll
in a beauty parlor), and making objects do what they are made to do.

Lacking 1   2   3   4   5   6   7   8   9   10 Demonstrates

Symbolic play refers to symbolic, or dramatic, play that occurs when
children begin to substitute one object for another, for example, using
a hairbrush to represent a microphone. The child may pretend to
do something (with or without the object present or with an object
representing another object) or be someone. They may also pretend
through other inanimate objects (e.g., has one doll pretend to feed
another doll).

Lacking 1   2   3   4   5   6   7   8   9   10 Demonstrates

Cooperative play refers to play where children plan, assign roles, and
play together. Cooperative play is goal-oriented, and children play in
an organized manner toward a common end. Moreover, cooperative
play is a "true social play" in which children cooperate or assume
reciprocal roles.

Lacking 1   2   3   4   5   6   7   8   9   10 Demonstrates

Sociodramatic play refers to play involving acting out scripts, scenes,
and plays adopted from cartoons or books. Children take/assume
roles using themselves and/or characters, like dolls, figures, and puppets, as they interact together on common themes. As a child matures
in play, themes, sequences, plans, problem solving, characters and
so forth become richer, and they begin to organize other children for
role-play.

Lacking 1   2   3   4   5   6   7   8   9   10 Demonstrates

Peer play refers to interactions with one's peers, which provide opportunities for physical, cognitive, social, and emotional development.

Lacking 1   2   3   4   5   6   7   8   9   10 Demonstrates

Constructive play is characterized as the manipulation of objects for the
purpose of constructing or creating something. Children use materials

to achieve a specific goal in mind that requires transformation of objects into a new configuration. LEGO pieces turned to cars or houses are examples of this play.

Lacking 1   2   3   4   5   6   7   8   9   10   Demonstrates

Representational play refers to pretend play, which emerges when a child begins to use familiar objects to represent their world; an example is a toy oven where food is being cooked.

Lacking 1   2   3   4   5   6   7   8   9   10   Demonstrates

Play categories in part from Psychology Glossary (2012),
www.psychology-lexicon.com

AutPlay Assessment of Play Skills

Please answer the following questions regarding your child's play. Try to think about specific times you have observed or played with your child and answer the questions as completely as possible.

Does your child play with toys?

Does your child play independently?

Does your child play with other children?

Does your child initiate play with other children or adults?

Do you have play times with your child?

Does your child interact with you during play times?

Does your child do pretend or metaphor play?

Does your child play with objects that would not be considered toys?

If someone (child or adult) asks your child to play, what does your child usually do?

Does your child seem to want to play?

Does your child's play seem age appropriate?

Describe your child's play.

AutPlay Unwanted Behaviors Assessment

Child's Name_____Age_____Gender_____Date_____

Please answer the following open-ended questions regarding your child's behavior. Try to recall specific situations and behaviors. If you are unsure, then leave the question blank.

1. Does your child seem to have sensory issues? If so, what type?

2. Does your child have behavioral "meltdowns" or unwanted behaviors?

3. What does your child's unwanted behaviors look like? Please describe actions, words, etc.

4. Are there specific times and or situations when you child is more likely to have unwanted behaviors? If so, describe.

5. Do you notice specific triggers that seem to create unwanted behaviors? If so, describe.

6. What is the typical intensity and duration of unwanted behaviors?

7. How frequently, in a week's time, does your child have unwanted behaviors?

8. Does your child have unwanted behaviors at school? If so, describe.

9. How do you currently address or manage your child's unwanted behaviors?

10. Does your child seem particularly dysregulated or "edgy" right after school?

11. Have you discovered anything that seems to help your child calm when he or she is having unwanted behaviors?

AutPlay Situation Behavior Assessment

Child's Name _____ Age _____ Gender ____ Date _____

Reporting Source for Assessment:

Parent Observation _____ Teacher Observation _____ Practitioner Observation_____ Other_____

Behavior (Describe the behavior, the intensity of the behavior, the frequency of the behavior, the duration of the behavior.)

_____

_____

_____

_____

_____

Situation (Describe where the behavior occurs, the place, the time, the people involved.)

_____

_____

_____

_____

_____

Antecedent (Describe what precedes the behavior, what is happening before the behavior occurs, what is happening in the environment, what other people are doing.)

_____

_____

_____

_____

_____

Consequence (Describe what the observed response to the behavior is, how other people respond, how the child's caregiver responds.)

Observable Intent (What appears to be the purpose of the behavior?)

Adjustments (What could be adjusted or modified that might help prevent future unwanted behavior?)

AutPlay Parent Self-Care Inventory

Please complete the following questions. Try to reflect on and think about each question and answer as thoroughly as possible. If you are unsure, leave blank.

1. Do you have support people in your life? If so, who and in what ways do they provide support for you or your family?

2. Are you involved with any community agencies or programs that provide support services? If so, what type of support are you receiving?

3. Do you have any leisure time that is child-free? If yes, describe the leisure time.

4. What do you do for relaxation?

5. What does self-care mean to you? Describe your current level of self-care.

6. What would be your ideal balance of childcare and self-care?

AutPlay Therapy Treatment Plan Profile
Instruction Sheet

The AutPlay Treatment Plan Profile is designed to help the practitioner create a treatment plan using the AutPlay Therapy approach. The profile helps practitioners organize and establish treatment goals, track the techniques being used, and track progress toward treatment goals.

Demographic information: This section is designed to collect basic demographic information on the client as well as identifying the practitioner completing the treatment plan and the date the treatment plan was created.

Presenting issues: This section is for recording presenting issues for which the client is coming to therapy. The majority of this data will likely come from parent reports both during the intake and from completion of AutPlay Therapy inventories.

Parent and child treatment expectations: This section is for recording the parents and, if applicable, the child's expectations from participating in treatment.

Previous evaluation/diagnosis and treatment history: This section is designed to collect information on any previous diagnosis the client has received where the diagnosis was acquired and who gave the diagnosis. This section is also for recording any previous psychological evaluation the client has received and who completed the psychological evaluation. It should also include previous treatments and/or therapy that the child has received.

Concurrent treatments/agencies working with child: This section is designed to collect information on what other treatments or therapies the client is currently attending and will likely be attending while he or she is participating in AutPlay Therapy. It is also designed for recording what other agencies or organizations are currently working with the client and family.

AutPlay Therapy inventories administered: This section provides tracking purposes for the practitioner. It records what AutPlay Therapy inventories have been completed and the date the inventories were completed.

Child/adolescent session tracking sheet: This section is designed to help the practitioner track what component area is being addressed and what play therapy technique is being used to address the component area. The date section provides opportunity to record when a specific technique was done. This section is usually completed each session with the new session information recorded. Some techniques may be repeated for several sessions; this section provides the opportunity to accurately record what is happening in each session.

Parent session tracking sheet: This section is designed to record what is being discussed and taught during the parent sessions. The information being presented to the parents and the date of the session should be recorded.

AutPlay Therapy Treatment Plan Profile

Child's Name	
Child's DOB and Gender	
Child's Diagnosis	
Parent's Name	
Practitioner's Name	
Date of Plan	

Presenting Issues

Parent and Child Treatment Expectations

Previous Psychological Evaluation/Diagnosis (where, when, who)
Treatment History (previous interventions)

Concurrent Treatments/Agencies Working with Child

AutPlay Therapy Inventories Administered

Inventory	Yes	No	Date Completed
Child Observation Form			
Child/Parent Observation Form			
Assessment of Play			
Social Skills Inventory			
Emotional Regulation Inventory			
Connection Inventory			

Child/Adolescent Session Tracking Sheet

Component Area Addressed (Emotional, Social, Connection)	AutPlay Intervention	Session Date

Child/Adolescent Session Tracking Sheet

Component Area Addressed (Emotional, Social, Connection)	AutPlay Intervention	Session Date

Parent Session Tracking Sheet

Training Content (Information Discussed, Interventions Taught)	Session Date

Parent Session Tracking Sheet

Training Content (Information Discussed, Interventions Taught)	Session Date

Additional Play-Based Autism Treatments

Replays

Replays is a fun, play-based, therapeutic approach to treat anxiety, emotional dysregulation, tantrums, and phobias and children who may have other diagnoses (e.g., autism, Asperger's syndrome, mood disorders, intellectual developmental disorder). Replays is based in the principles of cognitive behavioral therapy and adapted to a play-based format. Children cognitively from infancy through about a 10-year-old level can often benefit from this approach. Replays is described in the book *Replays: Using Play to Enhance Emotional and Behavioral Development of Children with Autism Spectrum Disorders*, by Levine & Chedd (2007) Jessica Kingsley Publishers. For more information, visit www.drkarenlevine.com.

Floortime

Floortime is a developmental, comprehensive program to promote healthy development and to help infants and children with a variety of developmental challenges, including autism spectrum disorder. Floortime is a specific technique where, for 20 or more minutes at a time, a caregiver gets down on the floor to interact with the child. Floortime is also a general philosophy that characterizes all daily interactions with the child. For more information, visit www.icdl.com and www.stanleygreenspan.com.

The Play Project

The PLAY Project was created by Richard Solomon, MD, in 2001 and is based on the developmental, individualized, relationship (DIR)-based theory of Stanley Greenspan, MD. The program emphasizes the importance of helping parents become their child's best PLAY partner. The PLAY Project has four key components: Diagnosis, Home Consulting, Training, and Research. For more information, visit www.playproject.org.

RDIconnect

The Relationship Development Intervention (RDI) Program for autism is a tailored set of objectives, extending from the Family Guided Participation Program and intended to target the core deficits of individuals with the diagnostic distinction, autism spectrum disorder. It is a comprehensive set of developmentally sequenced steps. The RDI Program for autism is committed to rebuilding the Guided Participation Relationship as the cornerstone for neural development. Families under the guidance of a certified consultant slowly and carefully construct opportunities for their child's neural growth while adding complexity. Over time, parents create a formidable impact on their child's ability to form reciprocal friendships, mature emotional relationships, conduct successful collaborations, and engage in flexible/adaptive thought and master problem-solving abilities. For more information, visit www.rdi-connect.com.

Autism Movement Therapy

Created by Joanne Lara, Autism Movement Therapy is an interhemispheric sensory integration technique incorporating movement and music in collaboration with positive behavior support (PBS) strategies to assist individuals with autism spectrum disorder in meeting and achieving their speech and language, social and academic IEP goals. For more information, visit www.autismmovementtherapy.com.

Social Stories

Developed by Carol Gray, a Social Story describes a situation, skill, or concept in terms of relevant social cues, perspectives, and common responses in a specifically defined style and format. The goal of a Social Story is to share accurate social information in a patient and reassuring manner that is easily understood by its audience. Half of all Social Stories should affirm something that an individual does well. Although the goal of a story should never be to change the individual's behavior, that individual's improved understanding of events and expectations may lead to more effective responses. For more information, visit www.thegraycenter.org.

Music Therapy

Music therapy is an established health profession in which music is used within a therapeutic relationship to address the physical, emotional, cognitive, and social needs of individuals. After assessing the strengths and needs of each client, the qualified music practitioner provides the indicated treatment including creating, singing, moving to, and/or listening to music. Through musical involvement in the therapeutic context, clients' abilities are strengthened and transferred to other areas of their lives. For more information, visit www.musictherapy.org.

Art Therapy

Art therapy is a human service profession in which clients, facilitated by an art practitioner, use art media, the creative process, and the resulting artwork to explore their feelings, reconcile emotional conflicts, foster self-awareness, manage behavior, develop social skills, improve reality orientation, reduce anxiety, and increase self-esteem. Art therapy practice is grounded in the knowledge of human development, psychological theories, and counseling techniques. For more information, visit www.arttherapy.org.

Pivotal Response Training

Pivotal Response Training (PRT) is a naturalistic behavioral intervention developed to facilitate stimulus and response generalization, increase spontaneity, reduce prompt dependency, and increase motivation while still relying on the principles of applied behavior analysis. PRT is child directed (as opposed to practitioner or parent directed), giving children the opportunity to initiate learning events. PRT works to increase motivation by including components such as child choice, turn-taking, reinforcing attempts, and interspersing maintenance tasks. For more information, visit www.koegelautism.com.

Integrated Play Groups

Integrated Play Groups (IPG) is a research-validated model originated by Pamela Wolfberg, PhD, in the late 1980s. The IPG model is designed to promote socialization, communication, play, and imagination in children with autism while building relationships with typical peers and siblings through mutually engaging experiences in natural settings. An IPG brings together children with autism (novice players) and competent peer partners (expert players) who are led by a qualified adult facilitator (IPG Guide). Each IPG is individualized as a part of a child's education/therapy program. For more information, visit www.autisminstitute.com.

Early Start Denver Model

Psychologists Sally Rogers, PhD, and Geraldine Dawson, PhD, developed the Early Start Denver Model. It is a comprehensive, behavioral early intervention approach for children with autism, aged 12 months to 48 months. The program encompasses a developmental curriculum that defines the skills to be taught at any given time and a set of teaching procedures used to deliver this content. This early intervention program integrates a relationship-focused developmental model with the well-validated teaching practices of applied behavior analysis (ABA). For more information, visit www.ucdmc.ucdavis.edu/mindinstitute/research/esdm.

TEACCH

TEACCH developed the intervention approach called "Structured TEACCH-ing," which is based on understanding the learning characteristics of individuals with autism and the use of visual supports to promote meaning and independence. Principles of TEACCH include understanding the culture of autism; developing an individualized person- and family-centered plan for each client, rather than using a standard curriculum; structuring the physical environment; and using visual supports to make daily activities understandable. For more information, visit www.teacch.com.

Creative Relaxation

Created by Louis Goldberg, Creative Relaxation incorporates yoga principles to improve behavior and focus, increase strength, flexibility, and balance, and promote self-regulation in children with special needs. Some of the principles and processes of Creative Relaxation include learning posture, breathing, mindfulness, and teaching postures selected specifically for children on the autism spectrum, with ADHD, sensory processing disorders, and emotional/behavioral disorders. It can be effective implemented in clinics, offices, and school settings. For more information, visit www.yogaforspecialneeds.com.

Building Blocks

The program utilizes an approach consistent with the Early Start Denver Model (ESDM). This newer approach incorporates components of ABA (modeling, positive reinforcement, and repetition) with components of Floortime (use of high affect, interactive play, and relationship building) and has been the subject of several significant studies supporting developmental and neurological progress in children with autism. The process includes assessing a child's current skills, identifies target behaviors (skills) to focus on the context of play, and designs and delivers each treatment session in a way that ensures the child is engaged, motivated, and provided with numerous opportunities to practice the selected skills. The therapist also provides coaching to parents, who are then able to incorporate the techniques in the family's daily routine. For more information, visit http://ne-arc.org/.

Brain Gym

Brain Gym describes a specific set of movements, processes, programs, materials, and educational philosophy. The main philosophy involves 26 Brain Gym movements, sometimes abbreviated as the "26." These activities recall the movements naturally done during the first years of life when learning to coordinate the eyes, ears, hands, and whole body. The 26 activities, along with a program for "learning through movement," were developed by educator and reading specialist Paul E. Dennison and his wife and colleague Gail E. Dennison who say that the interdependence of movement, cognition, and applied learning is the basis of their work. For over 20 years, clients, teachers, and students have been reporting on the effectiveness of these simple activities. Expected improvements in concentration and focus; memory; academics like reading, writing, math, and test taking; physical coordination; relationships; self-responsibility; organization skills; and attitude. For more information, visit www.braingym.org.

SCERTS

The SCERTS Model is a research-based educational approach and multidisciplinary framework that directly addresses the core challenges faced by children and persons with ASD and related disabilities, and their families. SCERTS focuses on building competence in Social Communication, Emotional Regulation and Transactional Support. It is applicable for individuals with a wide range of abilities and ages across home, school and community settings.

"SC" (**Social Communication**) is the development of spontaneous, functional communication; emotional expression; and secure and trusting relationships with children and adults.

"ER" (**Emotional Regulation**) is the development of the ability to maintain a well-regulated emotional state to cope with everyday stress and to be most available for learning and interacting.

"TS" (**Transactional Support**) is the development and implementation of supports to help partners respond to the child's needs and interests, modify and adapt the environment, and provide tools to enhance learning (picture communication, schedules, and sensory supports). For more information, visit www.scerts.com.

LEGO Therapy

LEGO-based social skills have been proven to be effective ways for children with social difficulties associated with autism, Asperger's syndrome, anxiety, depression, or adjustment disorders to improve their social interaction and communication skills. Improvements in social competence enable children to sustain lasting friendships and reach their highest potential. For more information see: *LEGO-Based Therapy: How to Build Social Competence through LEGO-Based Clubs for Children with Autism and Related Conditions* by Daniel B. LeGoff.

Apps for Autism and Developmental Disabilities

Meebie

This app assists children and adolescents in identifying emotions and various degrees of expression using the Meebie doll and several accessory pieces. Meebie provides a strong, engaging visual element to help with emotional regulation ability.

Touch and Say by Interbots

This app helps children learn various skills, such as colors, numbers, and letters, but also has an eye contact and feelings component. There is also a talk component where the app will mimic what the child says. This app is visually appealing and interactive.

Face-Cards

This app presents several different feelings that can be chosen, and an accompanying face is displayed showing the emotion. There is also an iGaze video that helps work on making and maintaining eye contact. The emotion faces are all female and provide good expressions.

Emotions Flash Cards for Kidz

This app presents several emotions categorized into three categories: positive, neutral, and negative. When a feeling is selected, a flash card showing an animated face displaying the emotion appears. This app offers a thorough index of emotion flash cards.

Autism Aide: Teach Emotions

This app focuses on the emotions of feeling happy, sad, hurt, ashamed, angry, bored, and scared. When a feeling is chosen, several different animated faces showing the emotions are displayed. There is an option to record someone saying the emotion word and an option to select background music.

Emotions (Teaching Tool for Speech and Language Development)

This app has five categories for helping with emotional regulation: 1) identifying pictures with emotions, 2) identifying emotions with a picture, 3) identifying picture-based scenarios with an emotion, 4) identifying pictures with labels based on scenarios, and 5) identifying pictures based on scenarios. Children are given options to choose from, and the pictures are of real people displaying emotions. This app is full of strong visuals and multiple ways to learn emotional regulation.

ABA Flash Cards

This app goes through several flash cards displaying real people showing emotions. When each flash card is presented, there is an auditory voice saying what the feeling is. The pictures are very good, and there are several feelings presented.

FeelingOmeter

This app uses a temperature gauge design to represent and help children learn about various feelings and levels of feelings. Children can choose from several feelings and choose colors to go with their feelings. Pictures can also be used to help display feelings. This app provides several elements that all combine together well to help children increase their emotional regulation ability.

Self-Regulation Training Board by Brad Chapin

This app helps children identify warning signs that correspond with a certain feeling, describes the feeling itself, and provides a strategy that the child can do when he or she is feeling the emotion. This app has strong visuals and seems appealing and engaging.

Zones of Regulation

This app is a thoroughly developed app that has several levels (reminiscent of popular video game design) and helps children learn about and develop emotional regulation ability. There are several components, and each one has strong visual elements and engaging levels for the child.

Stories2Learn

This app focuses on creating social stories. Several predesigned stories are available for viewing. The predesigned stories can be edited, and there is the option for creating your own social stories. This app is well designed and easy to use for making and viewing social stories.

Language Lab Spin & Speak

This app displays a board game that works on social skills. Up to 5 players can play at one time. This app addresses several social skills and is visually engaging and fun.

Choiceworks

This app includes working on emotional regulation, a waiting timer display, and a visual schedule. The components are all well represented and easy to follow with auditory prompts. There is a short accompanying book with each component.

FindMe

This app is designed to help children improve their social and attention/concentration skills. Several scenes are presented that become increasingly more challenging in identifying the target person in the picture while several distractions are happening.

Kimochis Feeling Frenzy

This is a fun, playful, and engaging app that helps children distinguish between positive and negative emotions and helps children identify various emotions. There are four different levels so children can begin on an easy level and progress to more challenging levels.

iTouchiLearn Feelings

This app presents several options for helping children learn about and identify emotions. There is a feelings section where children can watch a feeling being performed and identify what feeling was being displayed. There is a games section with various interactive games that work on feeling identification, and there is a music section that presents feelings through music.

Puppet Pals

This app presents several stages (scenes) to choose from and several different characters to choose from to create your own puppet show. Children can record the story using their own voice and then watch the story back. Practitioners can also record stories made specifically for children and have the children watch the stories. There is also a Puppet Pals II.

Story Maker

This app allows children to create their own stories with audio and pictures. Several pictures are provided, and personal pictures can be used. This app is easy to use with lots of options. Practitioners can also create stories designed specifically for the children they work with.

CBT4Kids

This app was developed by two clinical psychologists and provides a fun, engaging, and informative approach based on cognitive behavioral therapy. Practitioners can enter in actual children and track their progress. There are several interactive tools such as a relaxation and breathing game.

Time Timer

This is a simple but effective app. A timer is displayed that represents 1 hour. Users can select how much time they want put on the timer, and the time counts down with a red visual. This is very useful for parents and practitioners who want to use a strong visual aid to help children stay on task and understand amounts of time.

ZoLo

This app presents various shapes and sounds that children can manipulate to create fun and whimsical designs and play sculptures. There is a strong creative and sensory component that is very engaging.

Internet Resources

Toys, Games, and Supplies

The Self Esteem Shop, www.selfesteemshop.com
Child's Work Child's Play, www.childswork.com
Child Therapy Toys, www.childtherapytoys.com
Play Therapy Supply, www.playtherapysupply.com
Therapy Shoppe, www.therapyshoppe.com
Therapro, www.therapro.com
Fun and Function, www.funandfunction.com
Fat Brain Toys, www.fatbraintoys.com
The Sensory University Toy Company, www.sensoryuniversity.com
Toys for Autism, www.toysforautism.com
Discovery Toys, www.discoverytoys.net
Playability Toys, www.playabilitytoys.com
Special Needs Toys, www.specialneedstoys.com
The Sensory Spectrum Shop, www.sensoryspectrumshop.com
Autism Toys and More, www.autismtoysandmore.com
Autism Shop, www.autismshop.com
Different Roads, www.difflearn.com
Creative Therapy Store, www.creativetherapystore.com
Self Help Warehouse, www.selfhelpwarehouse.com
Toys of the Trade, www.toysofthetrade.com
Mind Ware, www.mindware.com
Young Explorers, www.youngexplorers.com

Organizations and Resources

One Place for Special Needs, www.oneplaceforspecialneeds.com
The Missouri Autism Report, www.moautismreport.com
Children with Special Needs, www.childrenwithspecialneeds.com
Liana Lowenstein, www.lianalowenstein.com
Autism Society of America, www.autism-society.org
National Autism Association, www.nationalautismassociation.org
HollyRod Foundation, www.hollyrod.org
Association for Science in Autism Treatment, www.asatonline.org
Families for Early Autism Treatment, www.feat.org
Autism Consortium, www.autismconsortium.org
CHADD, www.chadd.org
ADDitude, www.additudemag.com
National Fragile X Foundation, www.fragilex.org
FRAXA, www.fraxa.org
National Tourette Syndrome Association, www.tsa-usa.org
National Down Syndrome Society, www.ndss.org
Down Syndrome Research Foundation, www.dsrf.org

Apraxia-KIDS, www.apraxia-kids.org
NADD, www.thenadd.org
American Assoc. on Intellectual and Developmental Disabilities, www.aaidd.org
The ARC, www.thearc.org
Association for Play Therapy, www.a4pt.org
British Association of Play Therapists, www.bapt.info

References and Suggested Readings

American Psychiatric Association. (2014). *Diagnostic and statistical manual of mental disorders* (5th ed.). Washington, DC: Author.

Association for Behavioral and Cognitive Therapies. (2014). Available: www.abct.org

Association for Play Therapy. (2015). Available: www.a4pt.org

Attwood, T. (2007). *The complete guide to Asperger's syndrome*. Philadelphia, PA: Jessica Kingsley Publishers.

Autism Society of America. (2014). Available: www.autism-society.org

Autism Speaks. (2015). Available: www.autismspeaks.org

Barboa, L., & Obrey, E. (2014). *Stars in her eyes: Navigating the maze of childhood autism*. Mustang, OK: Tate Publishing.

Booth, P. B., & Jernberg, A. M. (2010). *Theraplay*. San Francisco, CA: Jossey-Bass.

Borgman, J. (2016). *Feelings Playing Cards*. Time Promotions.

Brady, L. J., Gonzalez, A. X., Zawadzki, M., & Presley, C. (2011). *Speak, move, play and learn with children on the autism spectrum*. Philadelphia, PA: Jessica Kingsley Publishers.

Bratton, S. C., Ray, D., Rhine, T., & Jones, L. (2005). The efficacy of play therapy with children: A meta-analytic review of treatments outcomes. *Professional Psychology: Research and Practice*, 36, 376–390.

Bundy-Myrow, S. (2012). Family Theraplay: Connecting with children on the autism spectrum. In Gallo-Lopcz, L., & Rubin, L. C. (Eds.), *Play based interventions for children and adolescents with autism spectrum disorders* (pp. 73–96). New York, NY: Routledge.

Centers for Disease Control and Prevention. (2015). Available: www.cdc.gov

Conner, B. (2007). *Unplugged play*. New York, NY: Workman Publishing.

Coplan, J. (2010). *Making sense of autistic spectrum disorders*. New York, NY: Bantam Books.

Corsello, C. M. (2005). Early intervention in autism. *Infants and Young Children*, 18, 74–85.

Cross, A. (2010). *Come and play: Sensory integration strategies for children with play challenges*. St. Paul, MN: Redleaf Press.

Dawson, G., McPartland, J., & Ozonoff, S. (2002). *A parent's guide to Asperger's syndrome and high functioning autism*. New York, NY: The Guilford Press.

Delaney, T. (2010). *101 games and activities for children with autism, Asperger's, and sensory processing disorders*. New York, NY: McGraw Hill.

Dennison, P. E., & Dennison, G. E. (1986). *Brain Gym*. Ventura, CA: Edu-Kinesthetics Inc.

Dienstmann, R. (2008). *Games for motor learning*. Champaign, IL: Human Kinetics.

Drewes, A. (2009). *Blending play therapy with cognitive behavioral therapy*. New Jersey: John Wiley and Johns Inc.

Exkorn, K. S. (2005). *The autism sourcebook*. New York, NY: HarperCollins Publishers.

Gallo-Lopez, L., & Rubin, L. C. (2012). *Play based interventions for children and adolescents with autism spectrum disorders*. New York, NY: Routledge.

Gil, E. (1994). *Play in family therapy*. New York, NY: The Guilford Press.

Gil, E. (2003). Family play therapy: "The bear with short nails." In Schaefer, C. E. (Ed.), *Foundations of play therapy* (pp. 192–218). New Jersey: John Wiley and Sons.

Greenspan, S., & Wieder, S. (2006). *Engaging autism*. Cambridge, MA: Da Capo Press.

Griffin, S., & Sandler, D. (2010). *Motivate to communicate*. Philadelphia, PA: Jessica Kingsley Publishers.

Guerney, L. (2003). Filial play therapy. In Schaefer, C. E. (Ed.), *Foundations of play therapy* (pp. 99–142). New Jersey: John Wiley and Sons.

Hull, K. (2011). *Play therapy and Asperger's syndrome*. Lanham, MD: Jason Aronson.

Jernberg, A. M., & Booth, P. B. (2001). *Theraplay: Helping parents and children build better relationships through attachment-based play*. New Jersey: John Wiley and Sons Inc.

Josefi, O., & Ryan, Y. (2004). Non-directive play therapy for young children with autism: A case study. *Clinical Child Psychology and Psychiatry, 9*, 533–551.

Kaduson, H. G. (2008). *Play therapy for children with pervasive developmental disorders*. Monroe Township, New Jersey: Heidi Gerard Kaduson.

Knell, S. M. (2004). *Cognitive behavioral play therapy*. Lanham, MD: Rowman and Littlefield.

Kuypers, L. (2011). *The zones of regulation*. San Jose: Think Social Publishing.

Laushey, K., & Heflin, L. J. (2000). Enhancing social skills of kindergarten children with autism through the training of multiple peers as tutors. *Journal of Autism and Developmental Disorders, 30*(3), 183–193.

Levine, K., & Chedd, N. (2007). *Replays*. Philadelphia, PA: Jessica Kingsley Publishers.

Lindaman, S., & Booth, P. B. (2010). Theraplay for children with autism spectrum disorders. In Booth, P. B., & Jernberg, A. M. (Eds.), *Theraplay: Helping parents and children build better relationships through attachment-based play* (3rd ed., pp. 301–358). San Francisco: Jossey-Bass.

Miller, M., & Smith, T. C. (2014). *101 tips for parents of children with autism*. Philadelphia, PA: Jessica Kingsley Publishers.

Moor, J. (2008). *Playing, laughing and learning with children on the autism spectrum*. Philadelphia, PA: Jessica Kingsley Publishers.

National Institute of Child Health and Human Development. (2014). Available: www.nichd.nih.gov

National Institute of Mental Health. (2014). *Early characteristics of autism*. Bethesda, MD: Author.

National Institute of Mental Health. (2015). Available: www.nimh.nih.gov

National Institute of Neurological Disorders and Stroke. (2015). Available: www.ninds.nih.gov

National Professional Development Center on Autism Spectrum Disorders. (2015). Available: http://autismpdc.fpg.unc.edu

Notbohm, E., & Zysk, V. (2004). *1001 great ideas for teaching and raising children with autism spectrum disorders*. Arlington, TX: Future Horizons.

Obrey, E., & Barboa, L. (2014). *Tic toc autism clock: A guide to your 24/7 parent plan.* Nixa, MO: Author.

O'Conner, K. J. (2000). *The play therapy primer.* New York: John Wiley and Sons Inc.

Odom, S. L., Horner, R. H., Snell, M. E., & Blacher, J. B. (2009). *The handbook of developmental disabilities.* New York, NY: Guilford Press.

Orlick, T. (2006). *Cooperative games and sports.* Champaign, IL: Human Kinetics.

Parker, N., & O'Brien, P. (2011). Play therapy reaching the child with autism. *International Journal of Special Education, 26,* 80–87.

Phillips, N., & Beavan, L. (2010). *Teaching play to children with autism.* Thousand Oaks: Sage Publications.

PsychCentral. (2014). Available: www.psychcentral.com

Psychology Glossary. (2012). Types of play in children. Available: www.psychology-lexicon.com

Ray, D. (2011). *Advanced play therapy: Essential conditions, knowledge, and skills for child practice.* New York: Routledge.

Respectrum Community. (2012). Child's development. Available: www.respectrum.org

Ross, R. H., & Roberts-Pacchione, B. (2007). *Wanna play.* Thousand Oaks, CA: Corwin Press.

Schaefer, C. E. (2003). *Foundations of play therapy.* New Jersey: John Wiley and Sons Inc.

Sensory Processing Disorder Foundation. (2015). Available: www.spdfoundation.net

Sherratt, D., & Peter, M. (2002). *Developing play and drama in children with autistic spectrum disorders.* London: Fulton.

Simeone-Russell, R. (2011). A practical approach to implementing Theraplay for children with autism spectrum disorder. *International Journal of Play Therapy, 20(4),* 224–235.

Siri, K., & Lyons, T. (2010). *Cutting edge therapies for autism.* New York, NY: Skyhorse Publishing.

Stillman, W. (2007). *The autism answer book.* Naperville: Sourcebooks, Inc.

Thornton, K., & Cox, E. (2005). Play and the reduction of challenging behavior in children with ASD's and learning disabilities. *Good Autism Practice, 6(2),* 75–80.

United States Food and Drug Administration. (2012). Available: www.fda.gov

VanFleet, R. (1994). *Filial therapy: Strengthening parent-child relationships through play.* Sarasota: Professional Resource Press.

VanFleet, R. (2012). Communication and connection: Filial therapy with families of children with ASD. In Gallo-Lopez, L., & Rubin, L. C. (Eds.), *Play-based interventions for children and adolescents with autism spectrum disorders* (pp. 193–208). New York, NY: Routledge.

VanFleet, R. (2014). *Filial therapy: Strengthening parent-child relationships through play* (3rd ed.). Sarasota: Professional Resource Press.

Vaughan, A. (2014). *Positively sensory.* Springfield, MO: Scribble Media.

Williams, B. R., & Williams, R. L. (2011). *Effective programs for treating autism spectrum disorder: Applied behavior analysis models.* New York, NY: Routledge.

Index

Lightning Source UK Ltd.
Milton Keynes UK
UKHW021240030120
356288UK00007B/100/P